McNamara v. Energy Dynamics, Inc.

Second Edition

McNamara v. Energy Dynamics, Inc.

Second Edition

Theresa D. Moore
Attorney at Law
University of California
Hastings College of the Law
Professor Adjunct
with
Patrick DePoy
Attorney at Law
and
Special thanks to Barkley Court Reporters
www.Barkley.com

Trial by Fire™ Case Series
Legal Advocacy with New and Modern Evidence

NITA®
National Institute for Trial Advocacy

Address inquiries to:

Reprint Permission
National Institute for Trial Advocacy
1685 38th Street, Suite 200
Boulder, CO 80301-2735
Phone: (800) 225-6482
Fax: (720) 890-7069
Email: permissions@nita.org

ISBN 978-1-60156-835-9
eISBN 978-1-60156-836-6

FBA 1835

Printed in the United States of America

Wolters Kluwer

Official co-publisher of NITA.
WKLegaledu.com/NITA

Contents

Acknowledgments

Thank you to attorney Patrick DePoy for his stellar work on *McNamara*. He has the instincts and the work ethic of a true trial lawyer. His energy, enthusiasm, and legal acumen are immeasurable, and it has been my honor to work with him.

Thank you to Court Reporter, Trainer and Educator Ana Fatima Costa for her graciousness and continual desire to aid legal education and for making it possible for us to include actual transcripts in modern format.

Thank you to Balinda Dunlap of Barkley Reporters for her tireless work in preparing *McNamara* transcripts after hours of reporting actual cases. Balinda has traveled all over the world working on cases of great import and is one of the best reporters I have ever worked with in my legal career.

Thank you to Facebook for permission for use in this casefile.

CASE SUMMARY

A community divided is at the heart of this case, a civil case involving toxic dumping. *McNamara v Energy Dynamics, Inc.* is a civil case for negligence pitting a local dairy farmer against a large energy company.

Defendant Energy Dynamics, Inc. specializes in hydraulic fracturing, better known as fracking, and came to Nita years ago to begin exploring for natural gas in the Columbia Shale. Energy Dynamics has developed a new chemical; this breakthrough unlocks precious resources, and untold millions of dollars, buried beneath a local community's feet.

But as McNamara experiences mysterious livestock deaths at his dairy farm, will the breakthrough prove to be a dangerous breakout of a toxic chemical? Either side can make a compelling case given the exhibits, testimony, and witnesses.

Author's Note

My purpose in writing the *Trial by Fire* series is to create challenging case files filled with options for students to work through and find ways out of a problem. Expect to extrapolate from the facts and "connect the dots" in working with the exhibits. All of the evidence is in the case file, but some evidence is more opaque and only reveals itself as the student becomes more immersed and educated on the case. As in real trials, problems exist, and students are expected to know the evidence rules and to develop unique strategies, theories, and themes to win their case. Strategy and creativity are important, and a neophyte student can be inspired to be creative, work hard, and win against an experienced and skillful trial student.

Don't be afraid to make the leaps of logic this case both inspires and demands. Prepare your witnesses using that logic, and enjoy the process.

Special Instructions for Use as a Full Trial

Issues for Trial

This case is tried on the issue of liability only, unless instructed otherwise.

This is a comparative fault jurisdiction, unless instructed otherwise.

Witnesses

Each side is limited to four witnesses, including adverse witnesses.

All witnesses are able to testify in English without an interpreter.

Witnesses for Plaintiff	**Witnesses for Defendant**
Sean McNamara	MK Phelps
Matt Barron	Lou Castrigano

Required Stipulations

All employees are agents of Energy Dynamics, Inc.

Energy Dynamics, Inc., is liable for the actions of its agents and employees.

Applicable Law

The applicable law is contained in the statutes and proposed jury instructions set forth in the case file. All years in these materials are stated in the following form:

YR-0 indicates the actual year in which the case is being tried (i.e., the present year);

YR-1 indicates the preceding year (please use the actual year);

YR-2 indicates the next preceding year (please use the actual year), etc.

Miscellaneous

Electronic exhibits can be found at the following website:

http://bit.ly/1P20Jea
Password: McNamara2

"The next move is always the test."

Seamus Heaney

THE U.S. DISTRICT COURT
FOR THE DISTRICT OF NITA CITY, NITA
Civil Division

SEAN MCNAMARA, McNAMARA INDUSTRIES,	)	
Plaintiffs,	)	CAL: YR-2-CIV-10886
v.	)	**COMPLAINT FOR DAMAGES FOR NEGLIGENCE**
ENERGY DYNAMICS, INC.,	)	
Defendant.	)	**DEMAND FOR JURY TRIAL**

COMES NOW, Plaintiff, Sean McNamara (Plaintiff), by and through the undersigned counsel, and makes this Complaint against Energy Dynamics, Inc. (ED). In support thereof, Plaintiff states as follows:

PARTIES

1. Plaintiff is an individual dairy farmer who at all relevant times herein resided in Nita City, Nita. Plaintiff is sole owner and chief operating officer of McNamara Industries.
2. Defendant ED is a corporation, authorized to do business in the State of Nita, which at all relevant times owned, controlled, and managed an energy corporation specializing in hydraulic fracturing for the extraction of natural gas in the Columbia Shale.

JURISDICTION

3. This Court has diversity jurisdiction over this action pursuant to 22 U.S.C. § 1332.
4. This Court has personal jurisdiction over Defendant ED pursuant to 22 U.S.C. § 1332.
5. This Court is the proper venue for this matter pursuant to § 6-202 (8) of the Courts and Judicial Proceedings Article of the Nita Code in that the cause of action that is the subject of this case arose in Nita City, Nita.

FACTUAL BACKGROUND

6. Since YR-15, Plaintiff Sean McNamara has owned the property at 24 Old Reservation Road, better known in the community as McNamara Dairy. Plaintiff and Plaintiff's parents have operated a dairy farm on the property since YR-65.
7. Defendant ED is a corporation, incorporated in Nita and Delaware on or about May 24, YR-13. ED specializes in hydraulic fracturing of shale rock for the extraction and capture of natural gas and other petroleum and hydrocarbon byproducts. ED has been conducting fracturing in the Columbia Shale region since January 1, YR-12.
8. Plaintiff's property abuts the Columbia Stream, and he has been using the Columbia Stream as a source of drinking water for his cattle and dairy cows for all time relevant to this complaint.

9. On or about April 12, YR-2, Plaintiff noticed his cattle and dairy cows exhibiting strange physical symptoms, including but not limited to lethargy, gastrointestinal problems, and neurological damage.

10. Between June YR-2 and July YR-1, twenty-five cattle and dairy cows belonging to Plaintiff died under mysterious conditions.

11. On or about June 20, YR-3, ED unveiled a new chemical that would lead to optimal extraction of natural gas through hydraulic fracturing. ED claimed the chemical, Tetrohydrocore ("Tetro"), had been lab tested for safety and was ready for use in the fracturing rigs throughout Nita.

COUNT ONE: NEGLIGENCE

12. Plaintiff restates and realleges each and every allegation set forth above as if fully set forth herein.

13. Defendant ED failed to properly test Tetro before introducing the chemical into its fracturing operations throughout Nita.

14. Defendant ED knew, or had reason to know, that Tetro would cause serious damage to the environment, specifically if leaked into drinking water sources in the area.

15. Defendant failed to adequately maintain waste pits for the collection of fracturing byproducts, including Tetro, in accordance with the State of Nita's Administrative Code. See 20 NAC § 25.001 et seq.

16. Defendant breached a duty of care owed to Plaintiff and similarly situated landowners in Nita by:

    a. Failing to properly test Tetro before introducing it into the field

    b. Failing to use reasonable care when constructing and maintaining its waste pits for fracturing byproducts and chemicals

17. As a direct and proximate cause of Defendant's breach of the duty owed, Plaintiff was harmed and damaged. Plaintiff's cattle and dairy cows and Plaintiff's rightful property were injured, harmed, damaged, or killed.

PRAYER FOR RELIEF

WHEREFORE, Plaintiff respectfully requests judgment against Defendant, that Plaintiff be awarded damages, and that Plaintiff be awarded restitution in an amount to be determined at trial, plus costs of suit, attorneys' fees, and such other and further relief as this Court deems just and proper.

Dated: November 1, YR-1

Respectfully submitted,

Aaron Q. Advocati

Aaron Q. Advocati
Attorney for Plaintiff

JURY DEMAND

Plaintiff, by and through the undersigned counsel, hereby demands trial by jury of all issues in this matter.

Dated: November 1, YR-1

Respectfully submitted,

Aaron Q. Advocati
Aaron Q. Advocati
Attorney for Plaintiff

THE U.S. DISTRICT COURT
FOR THE DISTRICT OF NITA CITY, NITA
Civil Division

SEAN MCNAMARA et al.	)	
	)	
	)	CAL: YR-2-CIV-10886
Plaintiffs,	)	
	)	
v.	)	ANSWER
	)	
ENERGY DYNAMICS, INC.	)	
	)	
Defendant.	)	

COMES NOW Defendant, Energy Dynamics, Inc., by and through the undersigned counsel, and makes this Answer to Plaintiff Sean McNamara.

PARTIES

1. Defendant is without sufficient information to admit or deny the allegations in ¶ 1 and, therefore, demands strict proof thereof.
2. Admit.

JURISDICTION

3. The allegation in ¶ 3 states a legal conclusion as to which no response is required.
4. The allegation in ¶ 4 states a legal conclusion as to which no response is required.
5. The allegation in ¶ 5 states a legal conclusion as to which no response is required.
6. Admit.

CLAIM FOR RELIEF: NEGLIGENCE

7. Defendant generally denies each and every allegation of the Complaint, and the whole thereof, and each and every allegation of each and every cause of action therein.
8. Defendant generally denies that its conduct directly or proximately caused the injury, illness, or death of the property of Plaintiff.

FIRST AFFIRMATIVE DEFENSE: ASSUMPTION OF THE RISK

9. Plaintiff knowingly and voluntarily assumed any and all risks associated with the use of Columbia Stream as a source of drinking water for his cattle and dairy cows, and such assumption of the risks bars in whole or in part the damages Plaintiff seeks.

SECOND AFFIRMATIVE DEFENSE: FAILURE TO MITIGATE DAMAGES

10. Plaintiff's alleged damages, in the death and injury to his cattle and dairy cows, are barred in whole or in part by Plaintiff's failure to mitigate such damages.

WHEREFORE, Defendant respectfully requests that the Court dismiss Plaintiff's claim, enter judgment in favor of Defendant Energy Dynamics, and award Defendant costs, attorney fees, and such other and further relief as the Court deems appropriate.

Dated: December 1, YR-1

Respectfully submitted,

Sam Porteral
Sam Porteral
Attorney for Defendant

EXHIBITS

Energy Dynamics, Inc.

PRESS RELEASE—June 20, YR-3

ENERGY DYNAMICS: LEADING THE WAY IN HYDRAULIC FRACTURING WITH TETRO©

Energy Dynamics has been an innovator in the field of hydraulic fracturing and natural gas extraction since its founding. Energy Dynamics has led the way in the search for clean, dependable natural gas to secure America's energy future. After years of development, testing, and retesting, Energy Dynamics is proud to announce another breakthrough in the field of hydraulic fracturing: Tetrohydrocore.

Dr. Matthew Barron and his team of chemical engineers deserve tremendous credit for this marvelous innovation in fracturing. Tetrohydrocore allows Energy Dynamics to capture up to 30% more natural gas during the fracturing process. Tetro is a synthetic hydrocarbon that attaches itself to natural gas particles that would otherwise be lost in the shale rock during the drilling process. No product like Tetro has ever been developed, and we're extremely proud of our team for this breakthrough.

Energy Dynamics prides itself on responsible extraction of America's natural resources. Tetro will not only allow Energy Dynamics to harness more natural gas, but will also ensure fewer byproducts of the fracturing process make their way into local aquifers and bedrock near drilling sites. Tetro is the future: a future where America's resources power innovation, protect our environment, and provide businesses with inexpensive local energy.

777 Main Street
Nita City, Nita 87004
555.555.0125
Fax 555.555.0145
www.edinc.nita

Energy Dynamics, Inc.

TESTING SUMMARY

Pursuant to instructions from Research & Development Supervisors, I have conducted tests on Tetro regarding its impact on water quality, diffusion rate through permeable and semipermeable surfaces, and impact on physiological functions of lab animals. The results of my experiments vary, but the effectiveness of Tetro as a capture-mechanism likely cannot be maintained without fundamentally changing the makeup of the chemical itself.

1. Water Quality

One of the primary advantages of Tetro is its relatively minor impact on water quality of surrounding surface water, and its inability to penetrate shale rock and bedrock to contaminate nearby aquifers.

Tetro has limited impact on water quality for the surrounding wells and water sources on which the chemical was tested. My team provided four drill sites with Tetro for natural gas capture. Each site saw a dramatic increase in natural gas capturing and reacted well with the dilute acid solution, disinfectants, and sand/granular products injected into drilled well bores. Because of its chemical makeup, Tetro does not break through the well bores into the surrounding shale, bedrock, and aquifers. Additionally, contrary to many additives, Tetro is non-corrosive and will not degrade the wells drilled to allow other additives.

WELL	Tetro (ppm)	Increase Productivity	Tetro Output (ppm)	Tetro Loss During Injection
Well 1	2000	34%	1861	6.95%
Well 2	2000	30%	1410	29.50%
Well 3	2000	31%	1908	4.60%
Well 4	2000	40%	1798	10.10%

This is a relatively small sample size. I recommend we continue testing wells and aquifers near drill sites to ensure continued effective recapturing of Tetro during extraction. I believe Well 2 was an outlier and further testing will prove that Tetro loss will be below 15 percent of Tetro injected into well bores. The increased productivity compared to the Tetro lost near well sites more than justifies the continued use of the chemical on site. Additionally, at present, there is no evidence that the Tetro lost made its way into aquifers or subterraneous water sources near sites. Until that time, there is no reason to believe that Tetro will have a negative impact on water quality. However, more testing should be done to make absolutely sure Tetro is not leaking into local water sources.

2. Diffusion Rate—Permeable/Semipermeable Surfaces

As with other byproducts, mostly water, Tetro needs to be stored properly in wastewater pits near or adjacent to bore well sites. Tetro is hydrophobic, and as such, is susceptible to escaping shallow pits through the topsoil and loose sediment. Shallow pits will suffice to trap Tetro, as with other well additives and contaminated water for retreatment after injection. However, testing shows that Tetro is likely to permeate all but the strongest pit linings. Concrete pits would be best, complete with polypropylene liners or equivalent in order to prevent leaking into topsoil and surrounding surface waters.

Additionally, due to potential hazards to wildlife and farm animals (see below), I recommend strong, possibly electrified fences near the pits. The water, and sheen from the surface of the water, may attract migratory birds that will be injured by the chemicals and unavoidable oil and gas slicks on water pits. With those precautions, there is very little likelihood that the Tetro injected will escape and impact water quality.

3. Physiological Functions—Exposure to Tetro

It is not entirely clear what physiological effects Tetro will have on farm animals, wildlife, and human beings exposed to the chemical in any significant way. We conducted limited tests in lab animals, including rabbits, rats, and chimpanzees. Over the course of sixteen weeks, we exposed each group of animals to a controlled amount of Tetro. As a control amount, we used 500 parts per million (ppm), which exceeded the Tetro loss in Well 2—the highest level of the test wells. In other words, we used the worst case scenario for exposure through lost chemicals to an aquifer or subterraneous water sources, but not necessarily the worst case scenario for spillage from wastewater storage pits. We felt this level was sufficient to determine the most likely impact of reasonable leaks into aquifers.

The results prove that exposure to Tetro causes many adverse physiological reactions, including hair loss; gastrointestinal complications; tumors; difficulty breathing; and neurological issues, including seizures, spastic movements, and temporary blindness. Exposure has also resulted in death for many of the animals tested. Additionally, several of the animals developed distinctive greenish-blue contusions near their abdomens, essentially strange bruising patterns not seen from exposure to other fracturing chemical additives. These results came from concentrated exposure to Tetro. Levels comparable to 500 ppm are very unlikely to occur in natural circumstances. That having been said, these results are alarming. Based on these test results, Tetro is dangerous to animal life. Human exposure could lead to serious medical complications that would expose Energy Dynamics to liability. As a chemical engineer, I realize the byproducts of hydraulic fracturing have dangerous properties when unleashed on the environment. Tetro is more dangerous than those known byproducts. This is not to say ED should suspend the use of Tetro—that decision is above my paygrade. However, I urge those in engineering and safety in the strongest possible terms to protect the public and the environment from exposure to Tetro.

Matthew Barron
Chief Chemical Engineer
March 15, YR-3

Exhibit 3

Energy Dynamics, Inc.

QUARTERLY GROSS WITHDRAWALS OF NATURAL GAS

Jan YR-6 through June YR-1
Million Cubic Feet per Drill Rig - Average

YR-6

AREA	N		Marcellus		Texas		N.Dakota	
Rep. Q	Gross	Change	Gross	Change	Gross	Change	Gross	Change
Q1	5.7	-	10.2	-	20.8	-	-	-
Q2	5.8	+0.1	10.7	+0.5	22.6	+1.8	-	-
Q3	6.7	+0.9	10.6	−0.1	22.9	+0.3	-	-
Q4	5.4	−1.3	11.1	+0.5	23.3	+0.4	-	-

YR-5

AREA	N		Marcellus		Texas		N.Dakota	
Rep. Q	Gross	Change	Gross	Change	Gross	Change	Gross	Change
Q1	5.8	+0.4	10.8	−0.3	21.0	−2.3	-	-
Q2	6.3	+0.5	10.7	−0.1	21.8	+0.8	-	-
Q3	6.6	+0.3	10.9	+0.2	22.0	+0.2	-	-
Q4	7.0	+0.4	11.1	+0.2	22.7	+0.7	-	-

YR-4

AREA	N		Marcellus		Texas		N.Dakota	
Rep. Q	Gross	Change	Gross	Change	Gross	Change	Gross	Change
Q1	6.7	−0.3	11.2	+0.1	22.8	+0.1	3.2	-
Q2	6.7	0	11.7	+0.5	24.0	+1.2	3.2	0
Q3	6.9	+0.2	11.0	−0.7	24.3	+0.3	3.4	+0.2
Q4	7.2	+0.3	11.0	0	24.3	0	3.9	+0.5

YR-3

AREA	N		Marcellus		Texas		N.Dakota	
Rep. Q	Gross	Change	Gross	Change	Gross	Change	Gross	Change
Q1	7.0	−0.2	10.8	−0.2	24.8	+0.5	4.0	+0.1
Q2	6.9	−0.1	10.4	−0.4	24.9	+0.1	4.2	+0.2
Q3	8.7	+1.8	13.6	+3.2	28.0	+3.1	6.0	+1.8
Q4	8.9	+0.2	14.2	+0.6	28.3	+0.3	6.3	+0.3

YR-2

AREA	N		Marcellus		Texas		N.Dakota	
Rep. Q	Gross	Change	Gross	Change	Gross	Change	Gross	Change
Q1	9.0	+0.1	14.6	+0.4	28.8	+0.5	7.0	+0.7
Q2	9.9	+0.8	14.7	+0.1	29.0	+0.2	7.2	+0.2
Q3	9.9	0	15.0	+0.3	29.0	0	7.1	−0.1
Q4	9.7	−0.2	15.2	+0.2	28.3	−0.7	7.3	+0.2

YR-1

AREA	N		Marcellus		Texas		N.Dakota	
Rep. Q	Gross	Change	Gross	Change	Gross	Change	Gross	Change
Q1	10.0	+0.3	14.8	−0.4	28.3	0	8.0	+0.7
Q2	9.9	−0.1	15.3	+0.5	28.5	+0.2	8.0	0
Q3	9.7	−0.2	13.6	+3.2	28.6	+0.1	7.6	−0.4
Q4	10.1	+0.4	14.2	+0.6	28.9	+0.3	7.5	−0.1

* The figures above were computed by dividing the total cubic feet of natural gas produced in each territory by the number of rigs operational at the end of each fiscal quarter.
** The North Dakota Region became operational with a group of ten well bore sites and rigs on February 1, YR-4.
*** The Location Names refer to the following areas:

A. N = Nita
B. Marcellus = Marcellus Shale, Pennsylvania, Ohio, and New York
C. Texas = Barnett and Palo Duro Shale
D. N. Dakota = Bakken Shale

NITA
Department of Natural Resources

CITATION

Date: May 13, YR-5	Address: ED Site, Old Rez Road
Operator: ED, Inc.	Citation: Pit Construction/Leakage

DESCRIPTION

On May 12, YR-5, Investigating Agent Logan Castrigano arrived at Energy Dynamic well head operation on Old Reservation Road. At location, south rig of grouping of three nearby, ED operates an active well, complete with multiple injection tankers present at time of inspection, flare out for chemicals, and a large pit for wastewater. Pit is close to the Old Reservation stream, approximately twenty yards. Pit is lined with large tarp, but tarp is not evenly spread. Clear violations of code, including but not limited to fences down near the pit, allowing animals or children to access wastewater. At least one dead bird present in the pit. Visible holes in parts of the tarp. Tarp is also the lowest grade polyurethane coating, no cement basin used, hoses leading to the pit completely in disrepair.

Spoke with foreman of the operation—he said it would be taken care of and that he knew the pit was in disrepair. Said he was waiting on management to authorize improvements, contacted contractors and subcontractors for bids to build a new pit, but was waiting for authorization from management. I told him this was inexcusable, and I had to issue a formal citation for violation, fine to be paid no later than ninety days after formal notice of citation by certified mail.

Logan Castrigano

Logan Castrigano
Field Inspector

Exhibit 5

To: PHELPS, MK
From: DRUMMEY, Tony
CC: BARRON, Matt
Date: June 15, YR-4
Subject: Tetro Breakthrough—TOP SECRET

Alright, let's all just calm down. MK, we will start working on the testing right away. I think what Matt meant to say is that we need to be professionals about this and not reach our conclusion (Tetro is safe) and then use science to back up the conclusion. We need to perform the right tests, see where they take us, and hopefully reach the right conclusion.

Thanks for your patience, MK

Tony

To: BARRON, Matt
From: PHELPS, MK
CC: DRUMMEY, Tony
Date: June 15, YR-4
Subject: Tetro Breakthrough—TOP SECRET

I would watch your tone if I were you, Matt. I appreciate the work you've done, but don't forget you wouldn't have gotten any of this if I hadn't been pouring money into your division all year—and don't think that even a scientist as talented as you are can't be replaced.

> *So let's have two wrongs make a right? You're asking me to rush a product to market because last year you and your team on Old Reservation had an epic screwup that could have caused major damage? I'm not prepared to rush something just so you can spin the story, MK. You focus on the business; I'll focus on the science.*

To: PHELPS, MK
From: BARRON, Matt
CC: DRUMMEY, Tony
Date: June 15, YR-4
Subject: Tetro Breakthrough—TOP SECRET

So let's have two wrongs make a right? You're asking me to rush a product to market because last year you and your team on Old Reservation had an epic screwup that could have caused major damage? I'm not prepared to rush something just so you can spin the story, MK. You focus on the business; I'll focus on the science.

To: DRUMMEY, Tony
From: PHELP, MK
CC: BARRON, Matt
Date: June 15, YR-4
Subject: Tetro Breakthrough—TOP SECRET

See! There ya go, Tony! I'm no chemist, but I have a vague sense of the carbonation process, and the bubbly will be flowing as soon as your team gives me the go-ahead for this product.

Matt, I'm not bullying you. I just have shareholders breathing down my neck looking for the next big break. I've gotten phone calls every day over the last year warning me that ever since the bad press we got last year, I need an answer. Can't keep giving them bad news, so let's get on it.

To: PHELPS, MK
From: DRUMMEY, Tony
CC: BARRON, Matt
Date: June 14, YR-4
Subject: Tetro Breakthrough—TOP SECRET

Gotta say I'm with MK on this one, Matt. I understand your concerns, and we need to test further, but there's just no reason to believe that this is going to behave the same way as arsenic or benzene in the field. It shares a few properties, but I don't think it will be nearly as damaging or carcinogenic in the environment when you understand the bonds it develops with natural gas.

I want more testing too, but MK, I am confident we can get this product to market within the next year while respecting the scientific process and protecting the public. Looking forward to popping the champagne!

Tony

> ***Again*** *with the Debbie Downer, Matt! C'mon—this is going to be the biggest thing since they discovered crude oil bubbling up in Texas!*
>
> *I am with you, we need to test it, but we cannot let cold feet stand in the way of an innovation that will lead to thousands of new jobs, more cheap natural gas, and a huge profit margin for this company. Let's do our due diligence, then let the world know we've reinvented the wheel!*

To: BARRON, Matt
From: PHELPS, MK
CC: DRUMMEY, Tony
Date: June 14, YR-4
Subject: Re: Tetro Breakthrough—TOP SECRET

Again with the Debbie Downer, Matt! C'mon—this is going to be the biggest thing since they discovered crude oil bubbling up in Texas!

I am with you, we need to test it, but we cannot let cold feet stand in the way of an innovation that will lead to thousands of new jobs, more cheap natural gas, and a huge profit margin for this company. Let's do our due diligence, then let the world know we've reinvented the wheel!

To: PHELPS, MK
From: BARRON, Matt
CC: DRUMMEY, Tony
Date: June 13, YR-4
Subject: Tetro Breakthrough—TOP SECRET

MK,

Pursuant to our meeting today, I wanted to remind you again: this is an amazing breakthrough, but we need to be cautious. There are still a lot of things we don't know about this chemical, and while I'm optimistic it'll be ready for the market soon, we can't rush these things. Hydraulic additives are already being blamed for all kinds of ecological disasters; we can't have anymore "blood" on our hands in the face of the environmental community.

I recommend you get me and Tony the resources we need to test this properly before we unleash it on the world. But you're right when you said today this was going to make us all rich—it will!

Particularly concerning—this chemical acts a lot like benzene and arsenic and has many of the same chemical properties. I won't bore you with the details, but if it acts that way in the environment, we created a gold-plated carcinogen. Not the end of the world, but we need to proceed accordingly. Let's start testing plans soon! HOORAY!

Matt

NITA
Department of Natural Resources

SITE INVESTIGATION

Date: February YR-3 Address: ED Site, Old Rez Road

Operator: ED, Inc. Citation: ____________________

CONCLUSION:

Chemical	MCL	Levels	Further Testing?
Benzene	5 ppb	2 ppb	N/A
Xylene	10,000 ppb	8,500 ppb	N/A
Arsenic	10 ppb	4 ppb	N/A

MCL: Maximum Contaminant Level
PPB: Parts per Billion
Set in accordance with EPA Standards and in accordance with the Dept. of Natural Resources

NITA
Department of Natural Resources

SITE INVESTIGATION

Date: August YR-3 Address: ED Site, Old Rez Road

Operator: ED, Inc. Citation: ______________________

CONCLUSION:

Chemical	MCL	Levels	Further Testing?
Benzene	5 ppb	4 ppb	N/A
Xylene	10,000 ppb	7,500 ppb	N/A
Arsenic	10 ppb	9 ppb	N/A

MCL: Maximum Contaminant Level
PPB: Parts per Billion
Set in accordance with EPA Standards and in accordance with the Dept. of Natural Resources

NITA

Department of Natural Resources

SITE INVESTIGATION

Date: February YR-2 Address: ED Site, Old Rez Road

Operator: ED, Inc. Citation: ____________________

CONCLUSION:

____

____

____

____

____

____

____

____

____

____

Chemical	MCL	Levels	Further Testing?
Benzene	5 ppb	4 ppb	N/A
Xylene	10,000 ppb	8,251 ppb	N/A
Arsenic	10 ppb	8 ppb	N/A

MCL: Maximum Contaminant Level
PPB: Parts per Billion
Set in accordance with EPA Standards and in accordance with the Dept. of Natural Resources

NITA

Department of Natural Resources

August 18, YR-4

Logan Castrigano
4501 City Hall
Nita City, Nita 57815

RE: Notice of Decision—Suspension

Dear Logan,

I am writing this letter to inform you that pursuant to our employment guidelines and relevant titles of the Nita Code, you are hereby suspended without pay for one week starting August 14, YR-4. After thorough review of the facts, I find that you violated your obligations as an environmental analyst and investigator. This letter shall serve as a formal notification of my decision and will remain in your personnel file for no fewer than five years, according to the Management Directives and the Collective Bargaining Agreement (CBA).

I have made the following findings related to the charges you face:

1. On the morning of July 18, YR-4, you were scheduled to inspect the hydraulic fracturing operation maintained by Nita Solutions (NS) in Fairview, Nita. Prior to your site visit, on July 9, YR-4, you called the foreman of the site, Lou Daniels, to invite him for coffee following the site visit. Shortly after your actual site visit on July 18, you went to coffee with Mr. Daniels at a nearby diner.

2. Your supervisor, Pam Boswell, informed me on July 24, YR-4, that she discovered this violation of your directives as an analyst and recommended further punishment. At a meeting to discuss these charges, pursuant to and required by the CBA, you offered the following explanation: You called on Mr. Daniels as a friend from college and not in your professional capacity. You never intended to tip him off to the visit and did not indicate you were going to be performing a site inspection or conduct testing of water and soil samples. You take responsibility for your action, but maintain there was nothing suspect about your conduct.

After reviewing the records, and having heard your side of the story, I respectfully disagree. The entire purpose of our operations revolves around the element of surprise. By giving operators advanced notice of our presence, or testing, we give them the chance to clean up their site for the few days we will be conducting inspection. I am sure it is not lost on you how disastrous it would be for the public health and our environment if major fracking operators knew exactly when, how, and by whom their inspections would take place.

To be perfectly frank, Logan, you know better than this. Since joining the DNR, you have come to understand that while we hope to work in harmony with the business community, sometimes we need to be adversarial. Providing advanced notice of inspections is one of the most awful violations of public trust I can think of at the moment. You realize that we have already been accused over the last several years of a certain coziness with industrial leaders, and your behavior does not help. I have also considered the fact that you do not deny the contact, but instead insist it was somehow "not a big deal." I could not disagree more strongly.

You have the right to formally appeal this decision in accordance with the CBA. You have the right to discuss this matter with your union steward, who may be able to assist you in composing a written appeal. You must turn in any written appeal within thirty days of the effective date of this decision.

I look forward to you rejoining the DNR after your suspension to better serve our community.

Regards,

Hank Hooper

Hank Hooper
Director
Nita Department of Natural Resources

Exhibit 8

NITA
Department of Natural Resources

December 10, YR-2

Logan Castrigano
4501 City Hall
Nita City, Nita 57815

RE: Removal from DNR

Dear Logan,

It brings me no pleasure to inform you that I have decided to remove you from the Department of Natural Resources, effective upon the receipt of this letter. You have consistently failed to issue citations properly for natural gas operators, and I am simply unconvinced it is because your subjects are behaving themselves.

It has been clear to me and your superiors for some time now that you do not share the commitment to the environment, community health, and public service required of your position. You are extremely talented and well-liked by industry leaders, but that may be the problem. The Department can no longer turn a blind eye to blatant favoritism on your part.

You have the right to formally appeal this decision in accordance with the CBA. You have the right to discuss this matter with your union steward, who may be able to assist you in composing a written appeal. You must turn in any written appeal within thirty days of the effective date of this decision.

The Department wishes you the best in your future endeavors.

Regards,

Hank Hooper
Hank Hooper
Director
Nita Department of Natural Resources

Exhibit 9

Text from Logan Castrigano to Lou Daniels

Exhibit 10

MORGAN L. SANTO
vetsrcool@santovets.com

321 Moose Track Rd — Phone: (509) 123-4567
Fairview, Nita 99163 — Cell: (509) 987-6534

EDUCATION

May YR-17	Doctor of Veterinary Medicine (DVM), College of Veterinary Medicine Nita University, Nita City, Nita
Licenses Held:	Nita, Washington, Florida
May YR-23	Bachelor of Science, Major—Husbandry, Minor—Chemistry Washington State University, Pullman, WA

RESIDENCY

Purdue University, Veterinary Teaching Hospital
Large Animal Surgery, May YR-17—YR-14

VETERINARY EXPERIENCE

Private Practice Veterinarian, Multi-Doctor Practice — 8/YR-7–present
Haven Clinic and Hospital, Mixed Animal Practice — *Nita City, Nita*

- Provide complete medical/surgical service primarily for competitive sport horses, cattle, sheep, dairy cows, hogs, and other livestock.
- Proficient in radiology, ultrasonography, endoscopy, reproduction, lameness evaluation, emergency medicine, and minor surgical procedures.
- Provide emergency and elective surgical services to the local veterinary and equine community on a part-time, shared and contractual basis.

Nita Zoological Society, Assistant Practitioner — 7/YR-14–6/YR-7
Nita Zoological Society — *Nita City, Nita*

Exhibit 11

Haven Clinic &
Animal Hospital

June 1, YR-4

Bureau of Animal Welfare
Department of Agriculture
4502 City Hall
Nita City, Nita 87005

To Whom It May Concern:

I am writing to lodge a formal complaint against Sean McNamara of McNamara Farms for animal cruelty and for failure to maintain conditions consistent with organic farming. I do so in my official capacity as a veterinarian and pursuant to my legal duties as a medical professional.

McNamara called me to his farm regarding a potential chemical exposure for his dairy cows. He told me a handful of his animals were exhibiting unusual symptoms including spasms, lethargy, difficulty giving birth, irregular bowel movements, and other troublesome symptoms. I visited the farm on May 24, YR-4.

I found the animals to be living in tight quarters, in tie stall pens not consistent with animal health, and certainly not consistent with organic farming standards. More troublesome, there were lesions on the sides of the animals as if they had been struck by their handlers. I found the handlers I dealt with to be rude, uneducated, and prone to anger. That gave me great concern, as dairy cows are stubborn and can lead those not accustomed to patience to fits of violence.

I do not have extensive evidence of abusive conduct, but do wish the Department to conduct a further investigation on behalf of the cows and on behalf of consumers. Please do not hesitate to contact me with questions. Thank you.

Sincerely,

Dr. Morgan Santo

Dr. Morgan Santo
Haven Clinic & Animal Hospital
42 Market Street
Nita City, Nita 87005

Exhibit 12

To: BARRON, Matt
From: PHELPS, MK
CC: DRUMMEY, Tony
Date: March 26, YR-3
Subject: Tetro Research

I appreciate both of your input. Matt, thanks for all the terrific work. We'll take all of this under advisement as we introduce Tetro into wells across Nita. I think that right now, no one has a better safety record that we do. ED is doing absolutely everything it can to make sure we're fracking safely.

Tony, thanks for weighing in. Again, I'll keep all of this in mind, and we'll make sure both of you can keep doing this important work as we go forward. Best

MKP

To: PHELPS, MK
From: BARRON, Matt
CC: DRUMMEY, Tony
Date: March 26, YR-3
Subject: Tetro Research

I see where you're coming from, Tony. Here's my only problem—these high levels of exposure are high for what we HOPE will be the case. In other words, yes, I want to keep Tetro levels low (though it's not benzene, so it doesn't have to be at benzene's lowest levels). However, what if there's a spill of the additives? What if a pit overflows—and we know that happens and has happened before, and we get high concentration levels into water sources?

I'm trying to plan for the worst, and as a scientist and *not a businessman*, I gave my opinion based on the data. If you had a problem during the experiments, you should have spoken up. You never said a word during the experiments, and now you are chiming in with your critiques of the studies. We're a team—start acting like it.

M

To: PHELPS, MK
From: DRUMMEY, Tony
CC: BARRON, Matt
Date: March 25, YR-3
Subject: Tetro Research

MK,

I am afraid I am going to have to respectfully dissent from Matt's conclusions, if not the overall premise of the study. You asked us to figure out the potential liability issues we as an organization might face if we sent Tetro into the market. I think Matt has wildly exaggerated the conclusions he reached.

1) Water Quality

I agree with Matt's conclusions that Tetro will not leak into local water supplies. I'd also like to note that in terms of testing the wastewater for Tetro remaining, we expect some loss because the whole point of Tetro is to latch onto and form bonds with the natural gas molecules released from the shale.

You have to figure that with the increased productivity, we're losing a solid 5 to 6 percent of the Tetro injected just to its natural process. Which is why Tetro is such a miracle—the high pressure in the bore wells creates a low probability of bonding because there is so much activity, but the Tetro molecules that do bond become more able to "grab" gas molecules as they get heavier. Think of them as magnets, and each time they get another "little magnet" of a gas molecule, they get more magnetized.

So yes, we're losing some Tetro, which might be going into the ground. However, a lot of that Tetro is getting "lost" because it's not part of the wastewater—it's part of the natural gas we're harvesting. I don't think Matt considered that here.

2) Diffusion Rate

We obviously need to make the wastewater pits as safe as possible, but nothing is ever perfect. We can't let the perfect be the enemy of the good. If Matt insists we have perfect pits before introducing Tetro, we will never introduce Tetro. I share the concerns, but just feel there is too much doom and gloom in this report.

3) Health Risks

Again, the concerns here are overblown. We exposed these animals to 500 ppb, which is 100 times the legally safe limit for benzene in water under Nita DNR guidelines. So yes, because this chemical shares characteristics with benzene, we found it has many of the same physiological effects of benzene. Therefore, can we be surprised that we expose them to such a powerful dose and they start growing third eyes and dying of terrible diseases? No, of course not. I still think Tetro could be dangerous because, again, it shares chemical properties with benzene, which is a fairly nasty carcinogen. I just think this study doesn't prove what Matt thinks it does and felt I needed to voice my opinion.

Matt, you know I respect you a great deal, but I just can't get on board with your naysaying when the future of this company, and in a lot of ways, this whole state are on the line.

Thanks,

T

NITA

Department of Natural Resources

May 30, YR-5

ENERGY DYNAMICS, INC.
Energy Dynamics Center
1 E. Industry Street
Nita City, Nita

<u>RE: Notice of Violation—DNR Reference No. BA1-8722</u>

Dear Mr./Ms. Phelps:

The Nita Department of Natural Resources issues this Notice pursuant to Section 25.800 of Title 20 of the Nita Administrative Code (the Code). You are hereby notified that the Department has found by preponderant evidence that Energy Dynamics, Inc., violated the Code at the natural gas and hydraulic fracturing site located at 88 Old Reservation Road, Nita City, Nita.

On May 12, YR-5, I conducted an unscheduled inspection of the Site pursuant to my authority under the Code. I observed and documented several violations of regulations designed to ensure wastewater from hydraulic fracturing injections do not contaminate the surrounding environment. Based on my observations, Energy Dynamics did not construct a wastewater pit, tank, or series of pits with sufficient capacity to contain all pollution substances and wastes used or produced during drilling. I find that Energy Dynamics was aware of the deficiencies, based on my interactions with the foreman of the site and other employees.

If you wish to contest the fine, or if you wish to request a conference with the DNR to discuss the violation, you may do so in writing within seven calendar days of your receipt of the Notice of Violation. If you have any questions or would like to schedule the conference provided for in the Notice, please contact me at (773) 555-4623.

Sincerely,

Logan Castrigano

Logan Castrigano
Field Inspector,
Nita Department of Natural Resources
4501 City Hall
Nita City, Nita

Enclosures:

Exhibit A

Pit with fences partially erected, improper tarp coverage

Exhibit B

Entrance to Old Reservation Road operation, Waste Pit on the South East side of the site, near Old Res. Creek

CITY OF NITA CITY

Jeffrey Gunderson, Mayor

March 11, YR-1

Town Hall Meeting

Nita City, Nita City Hall

TRANSCRIPT

The following transcript was prepared by the Nita City Department of Records. In accordance with relevant regulations and statutory guidelines, I, Mary Swanson, recorded to the best of my abilities the real-time verbal exchanges between the participants of the above captioned Town Hall.

This file represents an unedited version of real-time captioning, which should neither be relied upon for complete accuracy nor used as a verbatim transcript. The original of this file was produced in all capital letters and any variation thereto may be a result of third-party edits and software compatibility issues. Any person who needs a verbatim transcript of the proceedings may need to hire a court reporter.

Mary Swanson
Mary Swanson
Office of Records

Mayor Gunderson: Good evening, everyone. I'd like to call this meeting to order. First, I'd like to thank you all for coming tonight. I am looking forward to an open, frank, and most importantly respectful discussion of the issues we've heard about in the news recently. That last part is the most important. MK Phelps and others from Energy Dynamics have been so generous with their time, and I will not tolerate outbursts or rude exchanges from the audience. You'll all get to ask questions at the end, but Sheriff Onyiego and officers in here will have no problem throwing out rabble rousers (laughter from audience), so let's keep it civil. Without further ado, I'd like to welcome MK Phelps.

(Audience applause)

MK Phelps: Thank you, Mayor Gunderson. I just want to say that I'm so pleased to be here tonight. I have a brief presentation to go through, and then I'll let Tony Drummey get into some more technical aspects of what we're doing these days, but let me first start by saying how proud we at ED are to hail from the great State of Nita and the greatest city in the world, Nita City.

(Loud audience applause)

MK Phelps: We are proud to be from the great state of Nita. And as the leader in cheap, clean natural gas production, we take pride in being an engine of economic growth in our great state. For the last decade or so, ED has been a leader in our field and a leader in Nita. We've been at the forefront of exploring the Columbia Shale, this state's most precious natural resource. You can just ask Mayor Gunderson—it's like a bank bubbling under our feet.

(Audience laughter)

MK Phelps: I think Tony might have a more scientific description, but for our citizens, it's just a giant ATM sitting right under you right now.

(Audience laughter)

MK Phelps: All kidding aside, we have this resource. So how do we access it, and how do we use it responsibly with an eye towards not just jobs and growth, but also safety and protecting the environment? These are all concerns we have every day at ED, and it's why we lead the industry in safe, reliable fracturing practices. Because let's not forget, this is our community, too. We drink the same water, breathe the same air, and we're all in this together. That's why I know that while we want to supply America with clean energy, power our economy, and reduce dependence on oil, we have to do it the right way.

UNKNOWN: (Inaudible shouting) Stop the drilling in the—

Mayor Gunderson: Sheriff, can you get—

UNKNOWN: (Holding sign or banner) thousands of gallons of chemicals every day! Stop the drilling until we can—

Mayor Gunderson: The Hall will come to order.

UNKNOWN: (Inaudible) until the tests—

MK Phelps: All right, so that's one opposed to our operations, are we—

(Audience laughter)

MK Phelps: Mr. Mayor, I didn't know we were doing a voice vote tonight, but I can—

(Audience laughter)

MK Phelps: Like I was saying folks, it's all about doing this right. So how do we do it anyway? These days, you hear a lot of people saying that fracking is dangerous; fracking kills; fracking causes earthquakes. Here are the facts. Hydraulic fracturing is the process we use to access millions and billions of cubic feet of natural gas in the shale rock under Nita. As you can see, the process is fairly simple. We drill down just like any other rig, then drill horizontally into the shale formations. We inject our own fracturing compound, which is mainly water, into the wells to break apart the shale and access the gas. Then, we take the water and chemicals left over and place them in containment pits for processing later. The results are simple—millions of dollars in revenue for the state and city, thousands of good paying jobs, and affordable clean energy for Nita City and the world.

(Audience applause)

MK Phelps: I'd like you all to take a look at this slide right here. Not sure can make—I think it might be hard to see, but I'll give you the idea. Can you see it? All right folks, here's the bottom line. This chart shows that natural gas and shale gas isn't just the present, it's the future. These show that for years and years to come, natural gas and fracking will be adding jobs and pumping money into our economy. So I'd like you to think about that the next time you hear some of these people bashing ED. With that, I'm turning things over to one of our best chemical engineers, and a real genius, Tony Drummey.

(Audience applause)

Tony Drummey: Thanks, MK. Folks, I want to thank you all for coming tonight, and most importantly, I want to extend my gratitude for your patience while I get into some nerd talk here.

(Audience laughter)

Tony Drummey: So folks, I realize there are controversies surrounding not just fracking, but specifically a chemical I helped develop called Tetro. If you'll direct your attention to this slide, I'd like to highlight the facts about Energy Dynamics and our record. First, we at Energy Dynamics have never been written up for violations. Nita City and Nita make a lot of money writing up other companies in the area, but they've never made a dime from us. Next, it's important to realize that for all the problems associated with fracking, there's no greener way to power us into the future than natural gas. Fewer toxins associated with burning it, half the carbon dioxide emissions—I mean it's a miracle bridge fuel. Most importantly for this meeting, Tetro has never been proven by any reputable scientists to cause health problems. I want to repeat that. Tetro has never been proven to cause these problems. You can listen to the rumor mills and a few bitter people, or you can listen to science. Finally, I assure you that we're doing absolutely everything possible not just to test and retest Tetro, but to make sure our sites are careful, clean, and in full compliance with the Department of Natural Resources. With that, I'll turn it back to MK before questions.

(Audience applause)

MK Phelps: Thanks so much, Tony. So let me just summarize here. We at Energy Dynamics are here for you. We are members of this community just like everyone here, and we want to stay for the long haul. I see we've got a line at the microphone, so I'll take your questions now.

Citizen #1: Hi, my name is Fred, and I'm a technician at a rig operated by ED. I just want to say I've been with this company for eight years, and they're putting food on my table and helping me save for my kids to go to college. So when I hear people bad-mouthing this company, they're bad-mouthing me and this whole town.

(Applause)

Fred: I know we're here to talk about the environment, so I won't take up too much more time. But I just want to say that I'm part of this company. I take pride in my job, and the team I work with does, too. So I just—I mean, I get why we're here, but I want to be—because I see a lot of faces in here of other people who work for ED, and we got nothing to be ashamed of. I am proud of this company and proud of my job. So that's—

(Applause, clapping)

MK Phelps: Fred, I want—

Fred: That's all I've got to say. Thanks.

MK Phelps: And Fred, I want to thank you, and hearing that warms my heart. And we're proud of you and the work you do.

Citizen #2: Hi everyone, my name is Sue Clemons, and I live over in Prairie Woods in Nita City. I know this company brings us a lot of money, but I've just been really nervous about some of the things I've heard about fracking. There are documentaries out there where people have these, you know, videos of water getting set on fire. And I saw on *60 Minutes* or some other program that there are people getting nosebleeds, headaches, having internal problems in areas with lots of fracking. So Tony, can you—I just want to know if you can address that because—

(Applause)

Sue Clemons: I have raised my family here, and I don't want to leave. But I know you're too powerful to get rid of, and if you—if the choice is stay or hurt my family, I'm on the next train out of town.

Tony Drummey: Thanks for your question, Sue. I just want to go over some of your concerns. I don't think there have been any major studies done, that I'm aware of, linking hydraulic fracturing to major health problems. I think that what you have in Nita is a bunch of companies working double time to make sure we don't have any accidents or—

Sue Clemons: But those videos, I mean you can't—

Tony Drummey: Right, and Sue, I haven't seen the video you're talking about, but I'll address your concern. When we drill down deep in the ground, we pass through the aquifers that supply all of us water. And sometimes, when a company is sloppy or irresponsible, they don't capture the natural gas properly or their own chemicals leak into the water source. Any number of things can go wrong. But that's when a mistake is made; it's not a natural byproduct of the process. All we can do is work hard to prevent accidents, collect the chemicals that we're sending into the ground—mostly water and sand—and then ensure we're doing all we can to keep this community safe. I stand by our record, and I know MK does, too, and if there are problems in the future, we'll address them accordingly.

Citizen #3: Hi Tony and MK, my name is Matt Barron, and we know each other, go way back. I just want to say I find it absolutely unbearable to let you stand up there and lie to these people.

Tony Drummey: Matt, we haven't lied about—

Matt Barron: And to see you say that Tetro is safe, and ignore all of our own research.

(Crowd boos)

MK Phelps: Now, wait, hold—

Matt Barron: Because when you—

MK Phelps: Matt hold your, we should—

Matt Barron: You know what the research and my work shows.

(Crowd yelling)

MK Phelps: Hold on, one at a time. Matt, I'm going to let you talk, then I want you to let me talk. And folks, let's all play by those rules.

Matt Barron: Tony, you and I looked into this. Tetro is a unique chemical that bears many of the same properties as arsenic and shares several important characteristics as benzene, which we know is a dangerous, potentially deadly chemical. And we also know that we are not getting back from the drilling that we inject into the ground. My question to you is, where's the rest going?

Tony Drummey: Well, first of all, Matt, we aren't doing anything because you were fired. And second—

Matt Barron: Now wait a minute, you—

Tony Drummey: Second, I—

Matt Barron: That's completely ridiculous and—

Tony Drummey: Second, I—Matt, I let you speak, now it's my turn. Second, I know where it's going. It's binding to the gas molecules, it's helping us not lose gas to the process, and it's making the whole process more efficient. You know that, Matt, so stop with the cheap tricks you've done.

Matt Barron: Well—Tony, I think I'm a little more independent now that MK isn't making the payments on my BMW like yours, and so I think my experiments and findings are just as legitimate as yours.

MK Phelps: Matt, I really resent that. I gave you all the tools you needed for testing back when you were with ED. I am sorry things didn't work out with us, but that doesn't—

Matt Barron: They didn't work out because you—

MK Phelps: Don't smear the whole company because you're mad at me.

Matt Barron: MK, you fired me because I told you how dangerous this is. I couldn't care less about being fired; it's the best thing to ever happen to me.

MK Phelps: Well, us, too, Matt. You were always a real headache, and I'm trying to be classy here, but you were always a wimp, and if we listened to you, man never would have invented fire or the wheel or any—

(Laughter)

MK Phelps: Or anything else even remotely dangerous, so take your nonsense back to Green Works or wherever and—

(Booing, clapping)

Matt Barron: MK, that's fine. I just have one last question: what are you doing right now to test Tetro more than what we did back in the day?

MK Phelps: Matt, we couldn't make this thing safer if we spent a lifetime—I'd stake my reputation on it. And I do, just like I stake my reputation on our safety record.

(Applause)

MK Phelps: We've got time for one more question, so go ahead, ma'am.

Citizen #4: Yes, I just want to say that I've heard some wildlife have died near those pools with contaminants. How dangerous are those? What's in them? I only ask because my dog wanders around woods, and I want to make sure he doesn't drink from one.

Tony Drummey: You sure do, ma'am. This isn't like drinking from the toilet or—

(Laughter)

Tony Drummey: It's not good for him to drink from there. So here's what we do. First, we make sure the pools are as secure as possible. We line them with polyurethane, we have cement basins at some sites, and we make sure the water in there doesn't leak into the ground. Next, we make sure we fence the area off so most animals and kids and things can't just wander into them. But to be honest, no one is perfect, and you can't prevent every accident.

Citizen #4: Yeah, but have you heard of the birds and squirrels dying near them?

Tony Drummey: Of course, and that's because we've got some nasty chemicals in there. Not in high doses, really, but it's supposed to be kept out of the environment. And I can tell you—and MK can tell you this, too—there's nothing we take more seriously. I can't think of a single thing we can do to make these pools any safer.

MK Phelps: And ma'am, I have to say I agree with Tony. We have a review process in place; we make sure we're doing our job. Don't forget, if we screw up, the DNR is all over us. Nothing makes me madder than cutting a check to them because—

(Laughter)

MK Phelps: It's true, because not only is it embarrassing, but it's costly. We work real hard to prevent leaks or pool contaminants from escaping. We'll keep working hard for you.

Mayor Gunderson: Well, I want to thank our participants—it's been spirited. I want to thank all of you for your respect, and to those loud mouths, thanks for at least not cursing. Thanks, folks.

(Applause)

Exhibit 15

Energy Dynamics, Inc. PowerPoint Presentation

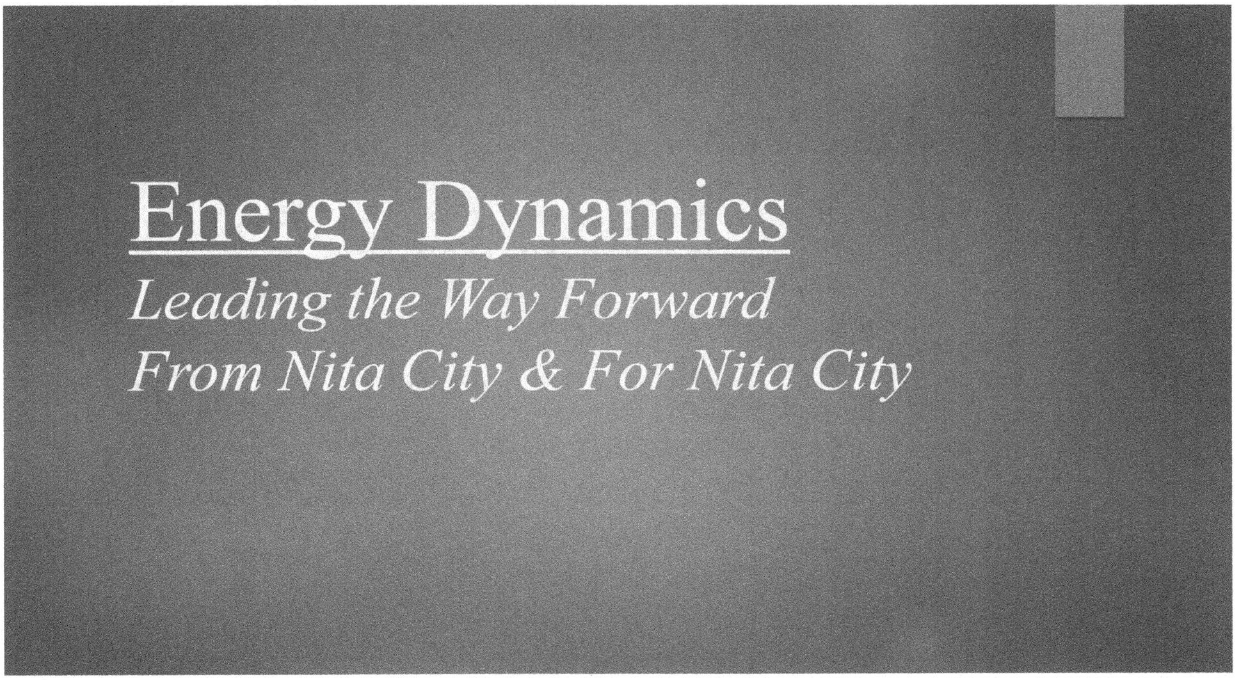

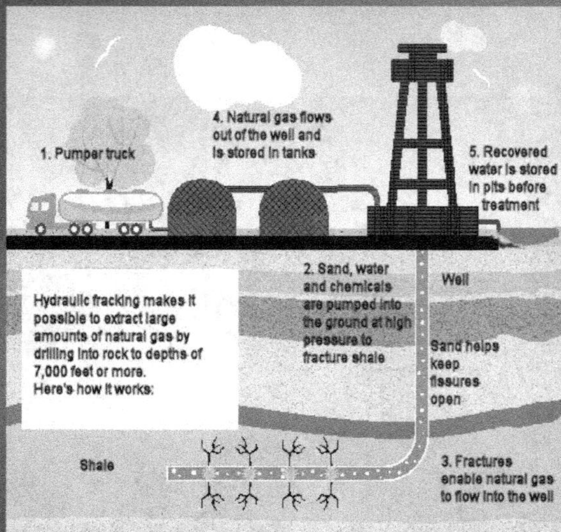

How Do We Do It?

1. Drill deep into shale formations below Nita City and the surrounding area
2. Pump water with important additives to harness gas locked in tight shale rock
3. Recover the gas that flows into the wells we've drilled
4. Store natural gas to be shipped around the country and across the globe
5. Safely store water and chemicals to be treated and reused in the future

THE BOTTOM LINE: JOBS, REVENUE,

AND CLEAN ENERGY

FOR OUR COMMUNITIES

Nita City: Our Home, Our Responsibility

- As a member of this community, ED takes seriously our responsibility to provide jobs and protect the environment
- Since 2000, ED has created thousands of good paying jobs for middle class workers in Nita City
- ED complies with all regulations related to our environment

It's not just our place of business, it's our home too

JOB CREATION – GROWING TOGETHER

- America is experiencing an energy boom unlike any we've seen in our lifetimes
- The Columbia Shale and others across the country are unlocking energy resources and leading to job growth for middle class families
- ED has added almost **18,000** good paying, permanent jobs
- Together, we're creating economic opportunity and expanding our middle class communities

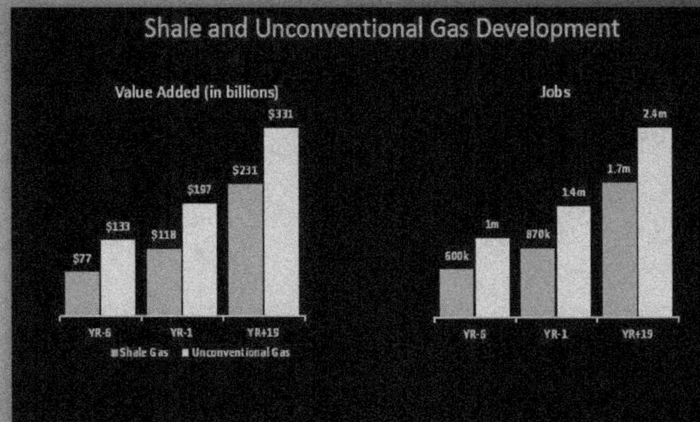

Natural Gas – A Greener Future for Children

- Recently, concerns have been raised about the safety of hydraulic fracturing and ED's cutting edge research and techniques.
- Here are the facts:
  1. ED has **never** had a major accident or spill at any of its drilling sites
  2. Natural gas burns **cleaner** than any other fossil fuel, reducing emissions and greenhouse gases to combat global climate change
  3. Tetro, an additive that helps us reduce waste, has **never** been proven to cause health defects or environmental contamination
  4. ED **continues** to test, improve, and retest all of our fracking additives

WE'RE HERE FOR YOU!

Questions? ***ASK US!***

Concerns? ***CALL US!***

Violations? ***LET US KNOW!***

This is our home, and we're here to serve you. We take pride in our relationship with Nita City, and hope we can continue our operations here.

Exhibit 16

***Petro Energy Monthly* Magazine Article**

PETRO ENERGY MONTHLY

Volume 30/Issue 6/June YR-3

A NEW LEADER

MK Phelps came up the old fashioned way: hard work, clean living, and a passion for innovation.

"I just thought the industry as a whole had room to maneuver," said Phelps, 49, in an interview shortly after the announcement of Tetro. The Stanford Business School graduate may not be the lab coat type, but her leadership has grown Energy Dynamics by leaps and bounds since taking the helm in June X-8.

HAS ENERGY DYNAMICS FINALLY SOLVED THE WASTE PROBLEM?

Shale rock is the new frontier of hydrocarbon energy. Over the last decade, there has been a natural gas boom the likes of which have not been seen since the Gold Rush of the mid-19th century. While ED has been a steady producer, a recent breakthrough may vault Energy Dynamics, and MK Phelps, to the top of the heap in the Nita natural gas wars.

HOW TETRO WILL CHANGE THE GAME

Q: How does Tetro work?

A: Essentially, the gas molecules we'd been losing to the process attach to the compound Tetro and we harness those molecules, would be escapees, into the process as normal.

Q: How long have you been developing this process?

A: We have one of the most high-tech R&D departments in the industry, which allowed us to develop Tetro at breakneck speed. That's how you need to operate in a market this dynamic.

Q: When will you begin seeing the results?

A: We fully expect Tetro to start making immediate contributions to our active well sites. As soon as we add Tetro to the fracking solution, we'll start reaping the dividends. We expect it to improve our yields per well by 30%.

"We developed this with breakneck speed. That's how you need to operate in a market this dynamic."

– MK Phelps

The development comes as welcome news for an organization mired by slow growth and disappointing exploration returns over the last several years. "It was tough answering to shareholders over the years," Phelps admits. "But with the development of Tetro, we expect to be the dominant player in Nita for years to come." The market already rewarded ED for its breakthrough, sending share prices higher and higher since the March announcement. Time will tell how much Phelps, and ED, top this breakthrough.

Exhibit 17

Old Red Barn at McNamara Farms website

PDF of exhibit follows this page;
webpage view available at:
http://www.nita.org/resources/MicroSites/mcNamara/bed-breakfast.php

Exhibit 17A

The Old Red Barn Bed and Breakfast at McNamara Farms website Home Page

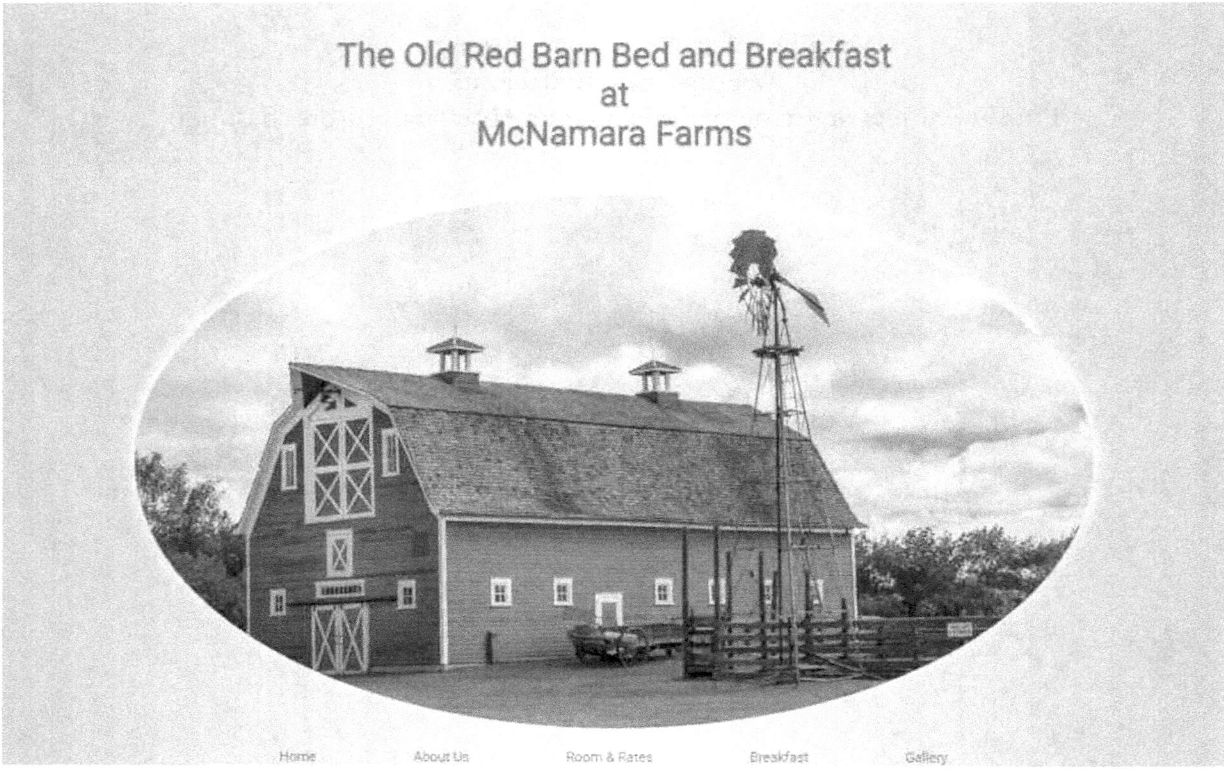

Exhibit 17B

The Old Red Barn Bed and Breakfast at McNamara Farms website
About Us Page

About Us

McNamara Farm has been a working dairy farm for more than forty years. The farm has been completely organic for more than a decade. After building a modern milking facility, the McNamaras converted the barn into a comfortable bed and breakfast with six cozy bedrooms, each with its own private bath. The farm continues to function as a dairy farm. Guests are welcome to visit the dairy barn and learn more about the day-to-day operation of the farm.

Home | About Us | Room & Rates | Breakfast | Gallery

Exhibit 17C

The Old Red Barn Bed and Breakfast at McNamara Farms website Reservations Page

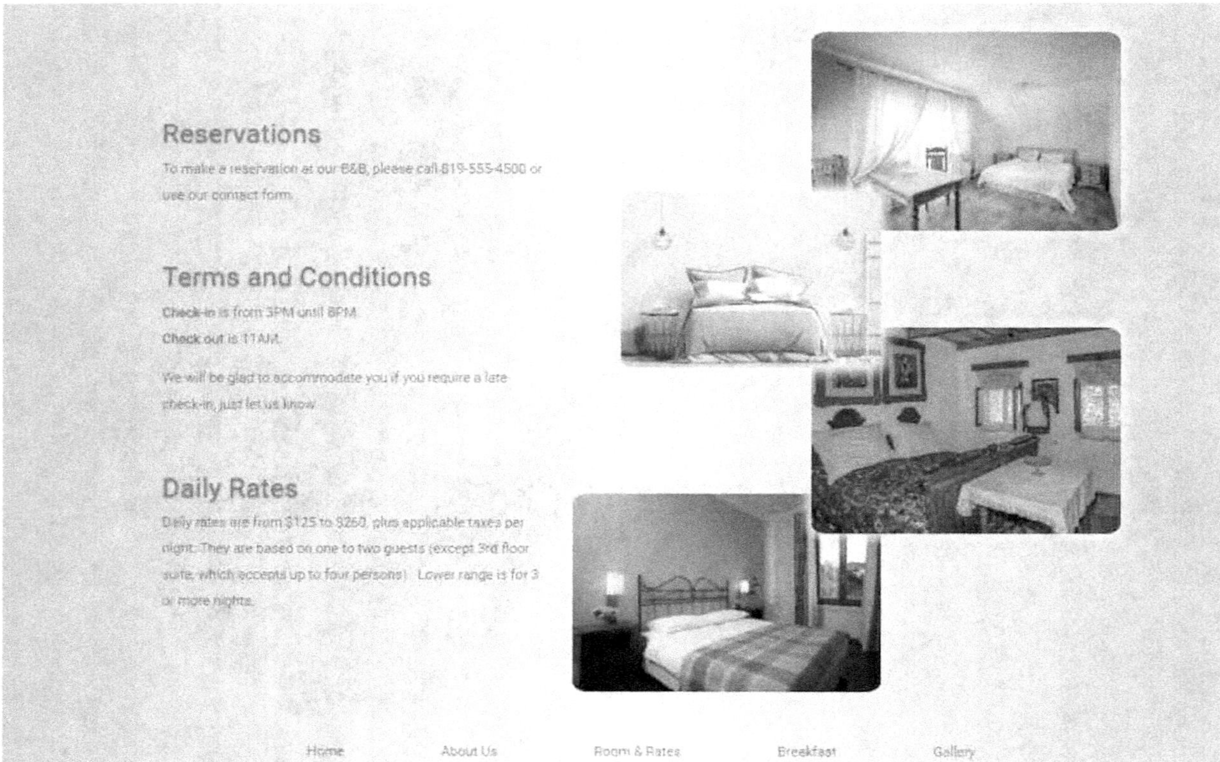

Reservations

To make a reservation at our B&B, please call 819-555-4500 or use our contact form.

Terms and Conditions

Check-in is from 3PM until 8PM.

Check out is 11AM.

We will be glad to accommodate you if you require a late check-in, just let us know.

Daily Rates

Daily rates are from $125 to $260, plus applicable taxes per night. They are based on one to two guests (except 3rd floor suite, which accepts up to four persons). Lower range is for 3 or more nights.

Home About Us Room & Rates Breakfast Gallery

Exhibit 17D

The Old Red Barn Bed and Breakfast at McNamara Farms website Breakfast Page

Breakfast is served every morning in the Old Red Barn kitchen. Hot service is from 7:30 until 10:00. If you are a late riser, a variety of fruit, cereals, pastries, and beverages are available until noon, with fresh fruit available throughout the day.

Join us at 5:00 every evening for wine and cheese. Our intimate happy hour will give you a chance to ask any questions you have about the farm and to get recommendations for area restaurants and attractions from the McNamaras and your fellow guests.

Home | About Us | Room & Rates | Breakfast | Gallery

Exhibit 17E

The Old Red Barn Bed and Breakfast at McNamara Farms website Gallery Page

Exhibit 18

Text from Sean McNamara to MK Phelps

Exhibit 19

Map of McNamara Farm

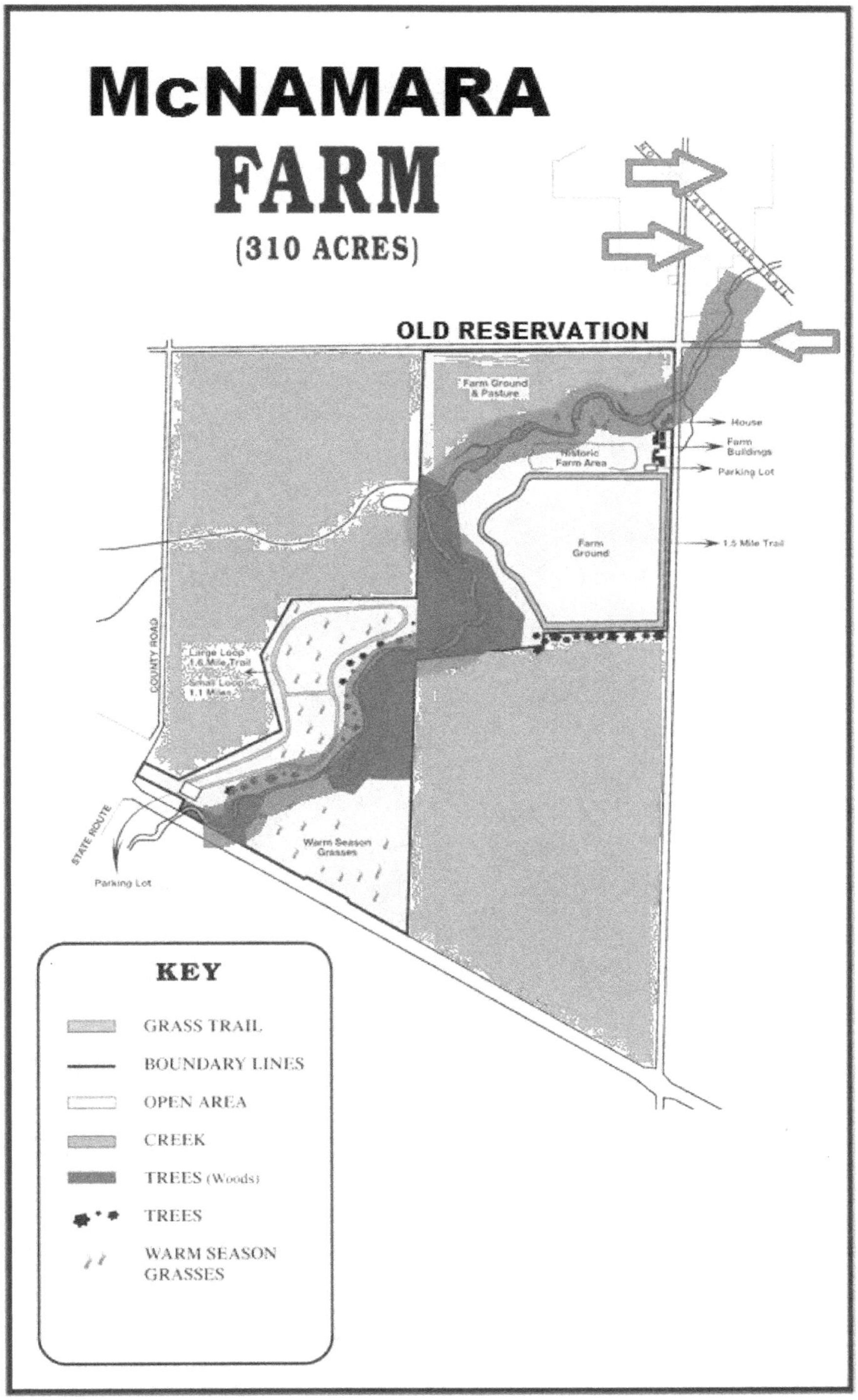

Exhibit 20

Veterinary Reports

General Submission Form

Haven Clinic & Animal Hospital

Nita City, Nita X0005
Phone: 773-555-0123
Email: morgan.santo@haven.nita

LAB USE ONLY

PLEASE NOTE: SAMPLES SUBMITTED OR TESTED BECOME PROPERTY OF THE ANIMAL HEALTH DIAGNOSTICE CENTER AND MAY BE TESTED AS PART OF STATE/FEDERAL SURVEILLANCE PROGRAMS

Reference No.** 87431BX

Submitting Veterinarian* M Santo
Clinic Name Haven
Address 42 Market
City, State, Zip
Phone No. 773-555-0123 Fax No. ( )
Submitting Vet's Signature [signature]

Owner Sean MacNa
Address 24 Old Res
City, State, Zip Nita City, Nita
Phone No. ( )
County ______ Town ______
NYS Premises ID N/A

HISTORY/CLINICAL INFORMATION: Please check all that apply

- ☐ Normal
- ☐ Hematological Hemorrhage
- ☐ Dermatological
- ☐ Fever
- ☑ Neurological
- ☐ Hepatic
- ☑ Gastrointestinal/Diarrhea
- ☐ Abortion/Repro Failure
- ☐ Endocrine
- ☑ Sudden Death
- ☐ Urinary/Urogenital
- ☐ Muskuloskeletal/Lameness
- ☐ Edema
- ☐ Ocular
- ☐ Neoplasia
- ☐ Chronic Weight Loss
- ☐ Production/Performance Decline
- ☑ Respiratory
- ☐ Anorexia
- ☐ Cardiac
- ☐ Erosion/Vesticular
- ☐ Other ______

Clinical/Differential Diagnosis: Severe symp of arsenic, benzene, petro?
Has related material been submitted previously for this animal(s)/herd ☐ Y ☐ N Accession No. ______
Date of onset of Herd illness ______ In animals submitted ______ Herd size: ______ No.dead 8 No. affected ?

Additional Info/History Worst yet. 8 dead on scene, handlers report same writings, DNR, urge Mac to restrict H_2O intake

ANIMAL IDENTIFICATION
SEX CODES: M=Male MC=Castrated Male F=Female SF=Spayed Female
AGE CODES: Y=Years M=Months W=Weeks D=Days DOB=Date of Birth

NO.	NAME/IDENTIFIED NO.	SPECIES	BREED	SEX	AGE
1	4836	Hol		M	1.0
2	1903			F	1.9
3	0054			F	3.5
4	6825			M	5.5
5	9910			M	6.1
6	0342			M	4.2
7	0967			F	4.1
8	7721			F	2.11
9	4946			M	1.10
10	3303			F	6.1

INDICATE *SPECIMEN TYPE* AND ANATOMICAL LOCATION (if appropriate): Ab Sore, Short breath; Second verse, same as 1st

DATE TAKEN: 7/6 YR-1

TESTS REQUESTED (per animal) ENTER FULL NAME OF TEST: No. 1, 9, 10 dead on scene; No 2, 5, 6, 7, 8 euthanized; No 3, 4 test, urinalysis, charcoal tabs(+) Fluids

Comments: Reaching epidemic

*The requesting veterinarian is responsible for tests, fees associated with this submission, and to notify the owner of test results

**If your internal reference No. is entered on this form, it will be used to identify this case on the test result form and on the billing statement (max 17 character field)

Page ___ of ___

General Submission Form

Haven Clinic & Animal Hospital

Nita City, Nita X0005

Phone: 773-555-0123
Email: morgan.santo@haven.nita

LAB USE ONLY

PLEASE NOTE: SAMPLES SUBMITTED OR TESTED BECOME PROPERTY OF THE ANIMAL HEALTH DIAGNOSTICE CENTER AND MAY BE TESTED AS PART OF STATE/FEDERAL SURVEILLANCE PROGRAMS

Reference No.** 87-43 BX

Submitting Veterinarian* M Santo
Clinic Name Haven
Address 42 Market
City, State, Zip
Phone No. (773) 555-0123 **Fax No.** ( )
Submitting Vet's Signature [signature]

Owner Sean Mc
Address 24 Old Res Rd
City, State, Zip Nita City, Nita
Phone No. ( )
County **Town**
NYS Premises ID N/A

HISTORY/CLINICAL INFORMATION: Please check all that apply

- ☐ Normal
- ☐ Hematological Hemorrhage
- ☐ Dermatological
- ☐ Fever
- ☐ Neurological
- ☐ Hepatic
- ☑ Gastrointestinal/Diarrhea
- ☐ Abortion/Repro Failure
- ☐ Endocrine
- ☑ Sudden Death
- ☐ Urinary/Urogenital
- ☐ Muskuloskeletal/Lameness
- ☐ Edema
- ☐ Ocular
- ☐ Neoplasia
- ☑ Chronic Weight Loss
- ☐ Production/Performance Decline
- ☐ Respiratory
- ☐ Anorexia
- ☐ Cardiac
- ☐ Erosion/Vesticular
- ☐ Other ____________

Clinical/Differential Diagnosis: ____________

Has related material been submitted previously for this animal(s)/herd ☐ Y ☐ N Accession No. ____________

Date of onset of Herd illness Fall Yr-2 In animals submitted ________ Herd size: _____ No.dead 5 No. affected ____

Additional Info/History Handlers report seizures, shallow breathing, fainting among dead. Some have GI issues again. Getting dangerous

ANIMAL IDENTIFICATION SEX CODES: M=Male MC=Castrated Male F=Female SF=Spayed Female AGE CODES: Y=Years M=Months W=Weeks D=Days DOB=Date of Birth						INDICATE ***SPECIMEN TYPE*** AND ANATOMICAL LOCATION (If appropriate)	DATE TAKEN	TESTS REQUESTED (per animal) ENTER FULL NAME OF TEST
NO.	NAME/IDENTIFIED NO.	SPECIES	BREED	SEX	AGE			
1	1971	Hol		M	4.1	Ab soreness,		Nos 1, 3, 4, 5, 7
2	2349	Hol		M	3.3	Fainting,		Deceased
3	2731	|		F	3.4	Inability to	1/15	
4	2789	|		F	2.9	stand,	YR-1	No 6 spasms
5	4613	|		M	1.11	vomiting		Fluid, Kao/Pect
6	4202	|		F	2.10			No 2 euthanized
7	6211	✓		M	4.10			Tox screens
8								same as last
9								
10								

Comments: Warned Mac to monitor diet

*The requesting veterinarian is responsible for tests, fees associated with this submission, and to notify the owner of test results

**If your Internal reference No. is entered on this form, it will be used to identify this case on the test result form and on the billing statement (max 17 character field)

Page ___ of ___

General Submission Form

Haven Clinic & Animal Hospital

Nita City, Nita X0005
Phone: 773-555-0123
Email: morgan.santo@haven.nita

LAB USE ONLY

PLEASE NOTE: SAMPLES SUBMITTED OR TESTED BECOME PROPERTY OF THE ANIMAL HEALTH DIAGNOSTICE CENTER AND MAY BE TESTED AS PART OF STATE/FEDERAL SURVEILLANCE PROGRAMS

Reference No.** 87-431BV

Submitting Veterinarian* M Santo
Clinic Name Haven
Address 42 Market
City, State, Zip
Phone No. 773-555-0123 **Fax No.** ( )
Submitting Vet's Signature [signature]

Owner Sean McNamara
Address
City, State, Zip
Phone No. ( )
County **Town**
NYS Premises ID

HISTORY/CLINICAL INFORMATION: Please check all that apply

- ☐ Normal
- ☐ Hematological Hemorrhage
- ☐ Dermatological
- ☐ Fever
- ☑ Neurological
- ☐ Hepatic
- ☑ Gastrointestinal/Diarrhea
- ☐ Abortion/Repro Failure
- ☐ Endocrine
- ☑ Sudden Death
- ☐ Urinary/Urogenital
- ☐ Muskuloskeletal/Lameness
- ☐ Edema
- ☐ Ocular
- ☐ Neoplasia
- ☐ Chronic Weight Loss
- ☐ Production/Performance Decline
- ☐ Respiratory
- ☐ Anorexia
- ☐ Cardiac
- ☐ Erosion/Vesticular
- ☐ Other

Clinical/Differential Diagnosis: Potential Arsenic Poisoning

Has related material been submitted previously for this animal(s)/herd ☐ Y ☒ N Accession No.

Date of onset of Herd illness Fall YR-2 In animals submitted ______ Herd size: ____ No.dead 3 No. affected ?

Additional Info/History Mac says handlers complained over summer of symp, but he thought no prob. Serious symp today

NO.	NAME/IDENTIFIED NO.	SPECIES	BREED	SEX	AGE	INDICATE SPECIMEN TYPE AND ANATOMICAL LOCATION (if appropriate)	DATE TAKEN	TESTS REQUESTED (per animal) ENTER FULL NAME OF TEST
1	Bess/8631	Hol		F	5/2	Yrs./Mo	Oct 30, YR-2	Nil Dead
2	3425	Hol		M	4/1	Abdominal soreness		No 2 + No 3
3	9130	Hol		F	4/0	some vomiting,		Tox. screen
4						Tired, low		urinalysis
5						mobility		CBC/Chem Panel
6								Fluids, Kaolin & Pectin
7								
8								
9								
10								

ANIMAL IDENTIFICATION — SEX CODES: M=Male MC=Castrated Male F=Female SF=Spayed Female; AGE CODES: Y=Years M=Months W=Weeks D=Days DOB=Date of Birth

Comments: Report results back to Mac

*The requesting veterinarian is responsible for tests, fees associated with this submission, and to notify the owner of test results

**If your Internal reference No. is entered on this form, it will be used to identify this case on the test result form and on the billing statement (max 17 character field)

Page ___ of ___

Exhibit 21

Facebook online profile of Matt Barron

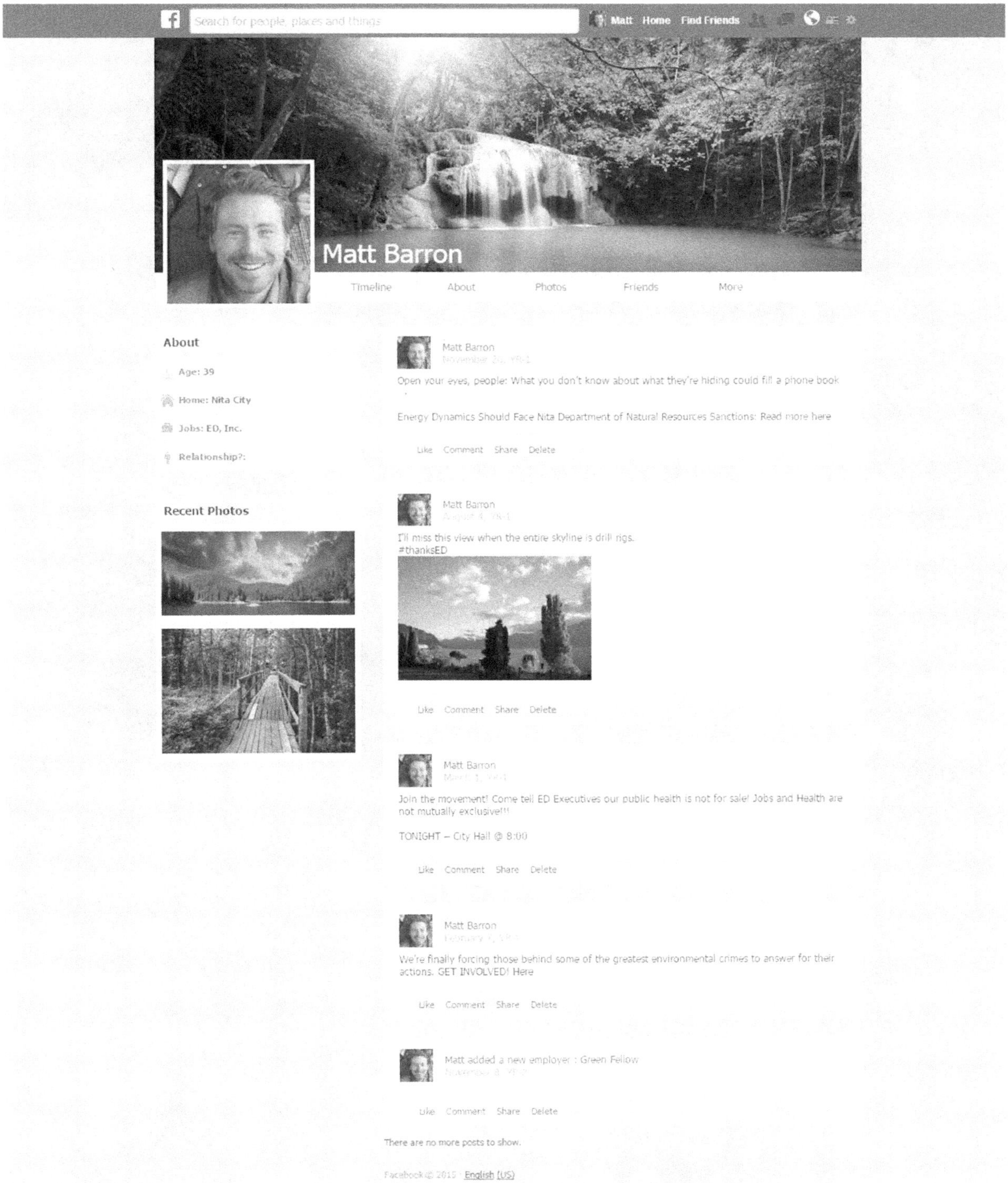

Photos of Dairy Cows

Exhibit 23

Deposition Transcript McNamara

Page 1

IN THE UNITED STATES DISTRICT FOR THE DISTRICT OF
NITA CITY, NITA
CIVIL DIVISION

SEAN MCNAMARA)
Plaintiff,)
vs.) CAL: YR-2-CIV-10886
ENERGY DYNAMICS, INC.)
Defendant.)

DEPOSITION OF SEAN MCNAMARA

Reported by: Nirelle Higgins, Student Court Reporter

Page 2

DEPOSITION OF SEAN MCNAMARA

BE IT REMEMBERED THAT, pursuant to the notice on, commencing at the hour of 2:00 p.m. thereof, at 24 Old Reservation Road, Nita City, Nita, before me, Nirelle Higgins, a student court reporter, there personally appeared:

SEAN MCNAMARA,

called for oral examination by counsel for the Plaintiff, who, after having been duly sworn to tell the truth, the whole truth, and nothing by the truth, testified as followed:

---o0o---

Page 3

EXAMINATION

Q. Please state your name for the record.
A. Sean McNamara.
Q. What is your occupation?
A. I am the owner and CEO of McNamara Industries.
Q. What business are you involved in?
A. Mainly dairy farms, but also organic farming.
Q. What kind of farming?
A. Well, we have one farm for walnuts, and another for cranberries in Michigan.
Q. How long have you been the CEO of the company?
A. I took over after my father passed away in YR-15.
Q. What was your occupation before taking over the company?
A. Well, right before I took over, I was the Chief Financial Officer, but do you mean other jobs I've had since--
Q. Well, how about just your general background. What was your first job?
A. Well, after graduating college, I started working for a brewery in Denver. I was their guy in charge of purchasing their hops and barley.
Q. What led you to that job?
A. I was an agriculture major at Columbia A&M, with a minor in agriculture financing. Wasn't sure if I wanted to

Page 4

trade commodities or get involved in farming. This job just seemed too good to pass up.
Q. How long were you with the brewery?
A. I started after I graduated in YR-22. I was there for four years.
Q. Where did you go after that?
A. A friend of my father's worked on Wall Street selling pork and wheat futures. He thought I would be good at it, so I gave it a try.
Q. How long were you in New York?
A. Three years.
Q. How did you enjoy that?
A. It was fine. The money was good.
Q. What made you leave?
A. There was an investigation in my firm. I was accused of insider trading on barley futures.
Q. Were you convicted?
A. I was never indicted. I cooperated with the SEC. A few of my coworkers received heavy fines, but I didn't.
Q. How was the situation resolved?
A. I don't even know. I cooperated and left New York after that.
Q. You never faced a conviction?
A. I mean, I did if I had been convicted. Insider trading is a serious accusation, but I was never convicted.

1 (Pages 1 to 4)

BARKLEY COURT REPORTERS

Page 5

Q. Why did you file this lawsuit?
A. Energy Dynamics polluted the streams near my grazing pasture, and I lost over two dozen dairy cows in a year.
Q. What do you mean "lost"?
A. They died.
Q. Naturally or were--
A. Well, no. Not naturally. They were poisoned, so that's not natural, I don't--
Q. No, I'm sorry, sir. I mean to ask did they expire on their own, or were they exterminated?
A. A few were exterminated. We put them down. Most died on their own.
Q. How were they put down when they were put down?
A. I called Morgan Santo, our family veterinarian, and he gave them a shot and did whatever he needed to do.
Q. Where is your dairy farm?
A. Our main dairy is at 24 Old Reservation Road. We have a few others around the state.
Q. How long have you operated the dairy?
A. The dairy's been in the family for decades. My father bought it with the inheritance from his parents.
Q. How large was the dairy when he bought it?
A. A few head of dairy cows. It was tiny.
Q. Did the farm make a profit?
A. You mean every year or--

Page 6

Q. Well, how about when he first started the dairy?
A. Of course not. The nature of the business is you'll lose money before you start making it. After a while, he turned a profit, started expanding, just like any business.
Q. Did your father expand beyond the farm?
A. No, he expanded within the farm. Buying more Holsteins, putting up the tie stall barn, then doubling the size. He turned it into a well-oiled machine.
Q. When did you inherit the farm?
A. YR-15.
Q. And before you were the CFO?
A. That's correct.
Q. What was the financial shape of the company when you took over?
A. Strong, but my father had expanded in a way that brought negative attention.
Q. What kind of attention?
A. Green Peace, or one of those other nutty groups, ran this documentary about how we were mistreating the cows we had, called our dairy an "animal sweat shop."
Q. How did they film the documentary?
A. They sent in this kind of undercover crew to film our workers.
Q. What did they find?
A. Well, they saw many of our employees hitting the cows,

Page 7

being a bit rough. It was a PR nightmare.
Q. What did do you?
A. Fired everyone involved. Changed the staff. I did interview after interview to explain our position. It didn't seem to be enough, so we went organic.
Q. What do you mean "went organic"?
A. Well, about 15 to 12 years ago, the organic food movement was really getting off the ground. We wanted to get in on the ground floor as a way of expanding, and as a way of purging the taint of that ridiculous documentary.
Q. Why was it ridiculous?
A. Because they're cows. They're not people. They weigh thousands of pounds. They're stubborn. You don't have to treat them like they're toddlers.
Q. But you fired your employees anyway?
A. We needed to do something. The press was killing us.
Q. How did you "go organic"?
A. Well, we stopped using growth hormones on the cows to get them to produce more. We started letting them graze out in the open instead of feeding them grain in pens. We pretty much tore down the old tie stall barn.
Q. How did that impact business?
A. It was expensive, but I had friends in the financial community that saw the potential for this as a business move and financed the transition.

Page 8

Q. So you took out loans to expand?
A. Yes, we bought more cows, and most importantly, we bought up all the land that now serves as our grazing pastures for the main McNamara Farm.
Q. How much was the loan for?
A. We had various financing agreements. All told, we took out about $50 million in loans from venture capital groups, major banks, other institutions.
Q. What is the balance on those loans today?
A. We've rolled them over several times. They're still part of our overall liabilities on our balance sheets, but the company is doing well.
Q. What did Energy Dynamics become a concern for you?
A. When they first started drilling in NC, I was thrilled.
Q. Why?
A. The natural gas industry is a big economic engine here. They've been a great company for a long time, and I'm pretty close friends with their CEO -- or I was.
Q. When did you begin having an acrimonious relationship?
A. Probably about four years ago.
Q. How did that come out?
A. Just north of our property, they have installed three of these rigs for natural gas. They're a terrible eyesore, and our farm has a pretty sizable tourist component.
Q. What kind of tourists come to the farm?

2 (Pages 5 to 8)

BARKLEY COURT REPORTERS

Page 9

A. We operate a bed and breakfast on the property. It's actually the old barn. These rigs were just obnoxious.

Q. What did you do?

A. I called MK Phelps and told her it wasn't going to stand. She told me to take a hike.

Q. When did you make this call?

A. September -- early September, of YR-5.

Q. Did you expect that reaction?

A. Yes, she was looking out for her bottom line. I wasn't really expecting her to stop, especially since it wasn't my property.

Q. How did it impact your business?

A. We saw a dip in reservations, but that's a small slice of our business model, so in the end, I let it go.

Q. How did the rigs ultimately impact your farm?

A. The first thing I noticed was a kind of sheen on the water in the stream, but it came and went.

Q. When did you first notice this?

A. Probably May or June of YR-4. This was right when they started, but it got better, and it got to the point where I couldn't see it.

Q. Did that sheen cause any problems?

A. A few of our cows got sick, so I called Morgan, our vet, to come check them out. Which was a total fiasco.

Q. Why?

Page 10

A. Morgan came and instead of doing the usual, blood samples, checking their abdomens, things like that, went on a little animal rights crusade.

Q. How do you mean?

A. Morgan came up to me and said, "Sean, those cows are in bad shape. I'm taking it to the DNR."

Q. What's the DNR?

A. The Department of Natural Resources. Their Animal Wellness Hotline where you report animal abuse.

Q. Why did he do that?

A. He said the cows looked malnourished. A few of them he said showed signs of abuse, and he said we should lose our organic certificate over it.

Q. How did you respond?

A. I told Morgan he was nuts, and that we treated those cows like royalty. Morgan started yelling at me that these cows deserved better and he'd see me in front of the DNR Board.

Q. How did that turn out?

A. It was ridiculous because I brought him there to handle the chemicals, and the sickness I thought they had, and there we were fighting about my organic certification.

Q. What happened?

A. DNR did a study. They said there was some evidence of abuse but not enough to lose my certification, so I paid a

Page 11

fine and called it a day.

Q. Did the cows get better?

A. Morgan gave me some medication. We patched things up eventually. I knew it was just part of the job.

Q. Did the cows improve from the medication?

A. Yeah, he said sometimes cows and other farm animals get into oil-contaminated water, and the drugs he gave me made a difference.

Q. Did the problems continue?

A. Yeah, the next summer, June and July of YR-2, we started seeing similar problems.

Q. Can you describe the cows?

A. I don't know, my handlers were telling me all kinds of things. They said they laid around all day, which didn't surprise me, they're cows. Then they told me a few were vomiting, and one of the new calves was having spasms.

Q. This all happened in June and July?

A. Oh, no. It started around then. The complaints started coming in, but they got worse over the summer and into the fall of YR-2.

Q. Do you have records of these complaints?

A. There are a bunch of emails that tell me what's going on. I can't remember all the problems.

Q. Did you know what the problem was?

A. No, the sheens on the water weren't there anymore, so I

Page 12

couldn't figure it out and neither could my staff.

Q. How did you handle it?

A. Come the wintertime, we called Morgan again to come on over.

Q. What was the answer?

A. We couldn't figure it out. Morgan said it was symptoms consistent with arsenic, but there was no arsenic in any of their systems.

Q. How did you respond?

A. I kept an eye on it, but at that point there was nothing I could do. I just had to wait and see.

Q. Did you stop letting the cows drink from the stream?

A. No, there was no reason to make them stop.

Q. Did you change anything about their diet?

A. Like I said, we were in a wait and see territory.

Q. When did you become aware of Tetrohydrocore?

A. Like I said, I'm a friend of MK Phelps, or was. When the company introduced Tetro, she was absolutely giddy about it and told me it was going to revolutionize natural gas in this country.

Q. When did you talk with her about this?

A. Regularly, a few times a month. She swore me to secrecy, and as a businessman, of course I kept it confidential.

Q. Did you ever ask her about when the chemical would be

3 (Pages 9 to 12)

BARKLEY COURT REPORTERS

Page 13

introduced?
A. I already had one insider trading investigation, I wasn't looking for another. I let her brag about how it would turn ED into the next Chevron, but didn't ask for specifics.
Q. When did you suspect there was something from ED causing these problems?
A. I had a conversation with Matt Barron at a town hall meeting.
Q. When was the town hall?
A. It was last year, March of YR-1. Matt was there and raising some serious Cain.
Q. What do you mean?
A. He's a firebrand, got sacked from ED and now fancies himself a crusader.
Q. What was he saying?
A. Well, Phelps was there explaining how ED was going to be expanding its drilling operation, and offering farmers and property owners a lot of money for exploration rights, and then she said everything would be perfectly safe.
Q. Did you mention your cows?
A. I am not some rabble-rouser. I didn't say anything, but Matt stood up and really embarrassed Phelps.
Q. What did he say?
A. That the new chemicals ED was going to use would start

Page 14

killing people, causing environmental Armageddon, just really going nuts.
Q. How did Phelps respond?
A. Called him a liar. Everybody went quiet, but Matt went nuts. You could just see his eyes, he was fired up. That's when he brought up the tests he ran that proved Tetro was dangerous.
Q. What did you think of this?
A. I felt bad for Phelps, but I knew my cows were sick, so I talked to Matt about it. He was getting huge cheers from the crowd, so I stepped up and said as an organic farmer, I was concerned. I couldn't resist the free publicity.
Q. What did Matt say to you in the conversation you had?
A. He told me Tetro, the new chemical Phelps told me all about, was going to cause serious problems for the environment.
Q. Did he go into details?
A. He told me to go to his blog to learn more. I told him I needed to hear more now. I told him my cows were dying as we spoke.
Q. How did he respond?
A. Matt said that wasn't a surprise. He expected more farmers to have similar problems going forward.
Q. Did you stop letting your cows drink from the stream?
A. No, I barely knew this guy.

Page 15

Q. What did you do?
A. Kept monitoring the situation, and as my cows started dying and having to be put down, I took him more seriously.
Q. Did you read his website?
A. His blog wasn't helpful. It was very over the top, and I couldn't take it too seriously.
Q. Can you go into specifics on the deaths of your cows?
A. Yes, the first three cows we lost in August YR-2. That was a very hot month, so I wasn't entirely surprised.
Q. How many cows do you have total?
A. At the farm or--
Q. Let's focus on the Old Reservation Farm; how many cows?
A. It's large. We have 200 head of cattle.
Q. How many cows die ever year just from natural causes?
A. I have no idea. Maybe a hand full.
Q. How do you have no idea?
A. Well, I'm the CEO. I don't run around the country counting heads of cows, that's not really my problem. I hire people to handle that, and when there are problems, they come to me.
Q. After that August, how many cows died afterwards?
A. That fall, about ten cows die. Was unbelievable. Young cows as well as old, which was the concern for our caretakers. That's when this was brought to my attention.
Q. What action did you take?

Page 16

A. Spoke to Morgan. That's when he told me there could be pollutants in the stream.
Q. When did you have that conversation?
A. The winter of last year, maybe January YR-1.
Q. Did things improve?
A. There were some more cows going down. I think my people were saying they had fewer new cases, but the cows with symptoms kept dropping like flies.
Q. How many did you lose that spring?
A. Maybe ten, on top of the cows we already lost that winter. It was awful. I finally stopped letting the cows use the Reservation Stream. We had to start shipping water in.
Q. How did you handle this?
A. I got in touch with Phelps, said ED should start paying for my costs, and I said I hoped it wouldn't come to a major lawsuit.
Q. Were you already thinking about suing?
A. I just lost 25 cows in a year, I was shipping in water to get these cows taken care of, paying ungodly vet bills. Yeah, I was thinking about suing. I'm a businessman.
Q. What did Phelps say?
A. Told me there was no proof. Matt Barron was a lunatic, and this product wasn't dangerous.
Q. How did you respond?

4 (Pages 13 to 16)

BARKLEY COURT REPORTERS

Page 17

A. I said I didn't want this to get nasty. I was ready to let bygones be bygones if Phelps and ED paid for the damage done, and started making sure the Tetro didn't get into my stream.
Q. How did Phelps respond?
A. Told me that any changes would be like stamping "guilty" on the front door, and that I had no proof about it besides one "vegan nutcase." Then Phelps said, "Look, if you thought it was so dangerous after the meeting, why'd you keep letting them drink there?"
Q. Did you think before that spring the rigs were to blame?
A. I might have, I don't know. It was on my mind, but I wasn't sure, but fixing it on a hunch would have been really expensive.
Q. More expensive than the veterinary bills?
A. I don't know, very expensive.
Q. When did you decide to bring this suit?
A. After meeting with Morgan and concluding the symptoms of the cows had to be from the rigs. Morgan basically ruled everything else out. Diet was fine, they weren't exposed to any other toxins.
Q. How could you be sure?
A. I'm not sure. I trust my vets. I have been in this business or a long time, and I know that these problems

Page 18

started happening once that chemical started going into the rigs.

Page 19

DEPOSITION REPORTER'S CERTIFICATE

I hereby certify that the witness in the foregoing deposition named,

SEAN MCNAMARA,

was by me duly sworn to testify the truth, the whole truth, and nothing but the truth in the within-entitled cause; that said deposition was taken at the time and place therein stated; that the testimony of said witness was reported by me, Nirelle Higgins, a student court reporter, a disinterested person, and was taken down by me in stenotype and transcribed through computer-aided transcription; and that the pertinent provisions of the applicable code or rules of civil procedure relating to the notification of the witness and counsel for the parties hereto of the availability of the original transcript of deposition for reading, correcting, and signing have been complied with.

And I further certify that I am not of counsel or attorney for either or any of the parties to said deposition, nor in any way interested in the outcome of the cause named in said caption.

IN WITNESS WHEREOF, I have hereunto subscribed my hand on July 28, YR-0.

Nirelle Higgins
Nirelle Higgins

Page 20

DECLARATION OF WITNESS

I, SEAN MCNAMARA, hereby declare that I have read the foregoing testimony, and the same is true and a correct transcription of my said testimony except as I have corrected.

Sean McNamara
Signature

July 28 YR-0
Date

5 (Pages 17 to 20)

BARKLEY COURT REPORTERS

Deposition Transcript Phelps

Page 1

THE UNITED STATES DISTRICT COURT OF THE DISTRICT OF
NITA CITY, NITA
CIVIL DIVISION

SEAN MCNAMARA,)
Plaintiff,)
vs.) CAL: YR-2-CIV-10886
ENERGY DYNAMICS, INC.)
Defendant.)

DEPOSITION OF MK PHELPS

Reported by: Nirelle Higgins, Student Court Reporter

Page 2

DEPOSITION OF MK PHELPS

BE IT REMEMBERED THAT, pursuant to notice, commencing at the hour of 9:00 a.m. thereof, at 42 E. Millennium Boulevard, Nita City, Nita, before me, Nirelle Higgins, a student court reporter, there personally appeared:

MK PHELPS,

called for oral examination by counsel for the Defendant, who, after having been duly sworn to tell the truth, the whole truth, and nothing but the truth, testified as follows:

---o0o---

Page 3

EXAMINATION

Q. Can you state your name?
A. MK Phelps.
Q. What is your address?
A. 42 Millennium Boulevard.
Q. What is your current occupation?
A. I am the CEO of Energy Dynamics, Incorporated.
Q. Can you describe the business of Energy Dynamics?
A. Yes, we are a leader in energy technology, extraction, and utilization. We're involved in every single phase of making America run.
Q. Can you be more specific?
A. Yes, we operate natural gas hydraulic fracturing operations across the continental United States. We also operate offshore crude oil drilling rigs in the Gulf of Mexico and the Eastern Seaboard. Finally, we're doing our best to lead the way in energy innovation and green technology.
Q. How much of your business is each sector?
A. You mean in terms of dollars and --
Q. Let's say last year's gross revenues. If you had to estimate the figures, what percentage did oil, gas, and green energy take up?
A. Okay. Well, we're a leader in natural gas extraction. I'd say natural gas sales accounted for 55-60 percent of our

Page 4

revenues last year, if I had to ballpark it. Crude oil and other petroleum from offshore operation made up most of the rest. Green energy is still a development area, and most of that is research and development.
Q. What is your dominant industry in Nita?
A. We only have natural gas operations in Nita.
Q. Can you describe the natural gas industry for us and what it entails?
A. Sure. Natural gas can be extracted really easily from deposits buried deep underground, just like petroleum and oil. But the U.S. does not have much typical natural gas. However, through the process of hydraulic fracturing, Energy Dynamics can extract billions of cubic feet of clean, safe, domestic natural gas.
Q. What is hydraulic fracturing?
A. It's the process of getting natural gas from very tight shale rock. The short version is that we blast highly pressurized water, chemicals, and sand into the ground, disrupt the rock, and unlock the natural gas down there.
Q. Is the process dangerous?
A. Not if done properly.
Q. How do you do it properly?
A. The biggest concern for us are the blowouts of the wells, safely and cleanly burning excess gas, and making sure the chemical by-products do not get into local aquifers

1 (Pages 1 to 4)

BARKLEY COURT REPORTERS

Page 5

and water sources.
Q. How do you prevent that?
A. We have the best engineers in the country working around the clock to man our rigs.
Q. What about the by-products?
A. It's important that we manage the by-products of fracturing. The high pressure unlocks not just gas but other chemicals deep in the shale rock. We need to make sure we keep that out of the environment.
Q. What kind of chemicals?
A. I'm just the CEO. I'm not the chemist.
Q. What kind of background do you have?
A. I graduated from Nita College in YR-20. Since then, I've been working in the energy industry and made my way up.
Q. Where else have you worked?
A. Right after gradation, I was in the accounting department at British Petroleum. I was there for five years.
Q. Where did you go after that?
A. I left the energy industry briefly and went to do venture capital.
Q. What did that entail?
A. Basically, working on Wall Street to pick good investments on behalf of investors and stakeholders in my

Page 6

company.
Q. Why did you end up there?
A. Well, they want to start investing in energy companies, and I had experience in the field. At least, they thought I had enough to make some sound investments.
Q. How long were you at the investment firm?
A. It was a venture capital group, and I was there for another five years.
Q. Where did you go from there?
A. I was briefly unemployed.
Q. Why?
A. The company fired me for a DUI arrest in June YR-10.
Q. When was your next job?
A. ED hired me in October YR-10.
Q. What was your position?
A. I came in through their Capital Investments Division. I was just an Assistant Vice President.
Q. How did you find out about this position?
A. My father was close friends with the head of the division, John Stevenson.
Q. What did you do for ED at the time?
A. I handled purchasing major equipment for them - drill rigs, tankers, other equipment. That kind of became my specialty.
Q. What kind of operations did ED have at the time?

Page 7

A. Small. We hadn't really become a leader in the industry yet.
Q. Did you already have gas-drilling operations?
A. Yes, we had purchased several plots of land from farmers in the area for exploration. Most of them were unsuccessful.
Q. What do you mean "they were unsuccessful"?
A. We didn't find the kind of petroleum and natural gas deposits that would have made for profitable operations - not until we discovered the potential of New Columbia Shale.
Q. When was that?
A. YR-8 or YR-9.
Q. How did business develop from there?
A. By leaps and bounds. We were one of the first companies using hydraulic fracturing, which at the time, we only tried down in Texas for various geological reasons.
Q. Were there safety concerns?
A. Always with an operation like ours, but as someone in the Capital Division, it was my job to buy the right products, the right materials, and the right safety equipment to ensure we did the job correctly.
Q. Where there any safety incidents related to the fracking?
A. Some town leaders were concerned about the chemicals we used.

Page 8

Q. What chemicals do you use?
A. I can't tell you that.
Q. Because you don't know or--
A. Well, I don't know all of them. Again, I'm not the chemistry kind of guy. But also because we don't have to tell anyone, and we don't want to because we have trade secrets on them.
Q. Was the town of Nita City making demands?
A. There were some investigative journalists poking their heads around. We mainly told them to mind their own business.
Q. How was the town reacting?
A. No complaints except a few rabble rousers and tree huggers. The jobs and the money flowing into the state were doing a lot of good.
Q. How much did you pay landowners for exploration rights?
A. Depending on the location, we're talking hundreds and thousands of dollars.
Q. But you don't have a figure?
A. It varied. We spent millions between YR-8 and YR-3, or YR-4 buying property and subterraneous rights.
Q. How did you end up becoming CEO?
A. Hard work and good ideas.
Q. I meant for the progression of time and events, what led to your promotion?

2 (Pages 5 to 8)

BARKLEY COURT REPORTERS

Page 9

A. **When a company grows as fast as ED, the people who were experienced got promoted. After we started developing the NC Shale, we tripled our workforce in Nita in just five years.**
Q. When was your first promotion?
A. **I became head of Capital Investments in YR-7, and then our CEO retired in YR-6. I was named CEO by the Board in April of YR-6.**
Q. When were you first alerted of the problems involved in this case?
A. **Matt Barron had been fairly confident Tetro would be a "miracle chemical" since he developed it, but he had concerns.**
Q. Did you mention them to outsiders?
A. **Of course not. I had a duty not to disclose that kind of thing.**
Q. When did you first hear from Sean McNamara?
A. **Sometime in the fall of YR-5. Maybe late summer. I can't remember.**
Q. What did he say?
A. **Told me that his customers were complaining about the noise. The rigs were an eyesore. Sean said people told him they'd never come back to stay at the bed and breakfast.**
Q. Did you believe him?
A. **I knew Sean, didn't think Sean would lie to me about**

Page 10

this. Also, it's a drill operation, so of course it's loud and not pretty.
Q. What did you tell him?
A. **I told Sean I'd bring it up with the right people.**
Q. Did you?
A. **No, I wasn't going to stop the operation because it bothered him.**
Q. Whose property are the rigs on?
A. **We have several wells on that property. It's owned by a small farmer, which I think also bothered Sean.**
Q. Why?
A. **Ever since Sean went "organic,"**
(Witness making hand gestures indicating quotations.)
he's been buying up small farms and diaries all over the place.
Q. Did McNamara try to buy this farm?
A. **Sean made an offer. The farmer told him very colorfully what he could do with the offer, and they've been nasty to each other ever since.**
Q. What does the operation on this property consist of?
A. **Like all of our operations, there are several well springs from which natural gas escapes. There's the drill rig, which bores into the ground and allows us to inject the chemicals to unlock the gas. Then, we have a dumping pit to**

Page 11

get the refuse.
Q. But there are multiple rigs?
A. **Yes, they're in close proximity to one another.**
Q. How close?
A. **I don't know.**
Q. Ten feet? Fifty feet?
A. **Somewhere in between.**
Q. Describe the waste pit.
A. **The entire fracking operation requires a tremendous amount of water. One of the things I purchased all the time with the Capital Section were water tankers. Just trucks to bring in water which we mix with chemicals to unlock the gas. What goes down -- a lot comes back up, and it has to go somewhere. The pits are lined with propyurethal or propypente or whatever. Again, not a chemist. That prevents the water and chemicals from leaking out.**
Q. How deep is the pit?
A. **Depends, but some can be very deep. The size of a major swimming pool.**
Q. How deep was this pit?
A. **Large. I believe it was six feet by twenty feet, and eight feet deep. It literally had to handle thousands of gallons of water and chemicals.**
Q. What is the hazard that comes with this?
A. **For any pit, it's about the chemicals and water seeping**

Page 12

into aquifers and contaminating well water. There were all these tree huggers that filmed videos of people lighting their tap water on fire and blaming it on the fracking operations.
Q. Do you know if they were to blame?
A. **I don't believe they were.**
Q. But you don't know for sure?
A. **It could have been a lot of things.**
Q. How do you prevent leaks?
A. **Lining the pits to prevent leaks and making them deep enough so that when it rains they don't overflow.**
Q. Did that happen in this case near McNamara's farm?
A. **He certainly thinks so, but I couldn't tell you. I'm not there twenty-four hours a day.**
Q. Are there any inspections of these sites?
A. **Of course. The Nita inspectors are on us all the time, and we welcome it. We want to be safe.**
Q. How often do they inspect sites?
A. **They are random and unannounced, but we have a good relationship with many of the inspectors.**
Q. What kind of comments did you receive from inspectors about your sites?
A. **Universally, great comments. They told us we were the best in the industry at complying with regulations.**
Q. Were you ever issued citations for failure to comply?

3 (Pages 9 to 12)

BARKLEY COURT REPORTERS

Page 13

A. A few times, but we developed almost 1,000 wells over the course of seven or eight years. Nobody's perfect.
Q. What were the consequences?
A. We paid fines to the State of Nita. A few wells were suspended.
Q. How many times?
A. Since I became CEO, we have only been issued three citations, and two were fairly minor.
Q. When were they issued?
A. I can't remember. A few months apart over the span of a few years.
Q. What about the site in question?
A. We got a warning related to our pit depth. The official citation was for potential to contaminate state water sources or something.
Q. When was this citation?
A. April or May of YR-6.
Q. What actions did you take?
A. We made sure the pits were properly sealed off -- that we had a proper depth. I made sure that these pits were as safe as possible.
Q. And were they?
A. Yes, they were as safe as we could make them at that time.
Q. When did you announce the first use of Tetro?

Page 14

A. We had a press release after I spoke with Matt Barron. This was going to revolutionize the industry.
Q. When was the press release?
A. Summer of YR-3.
Q. What reports did you receive before the release?
A. We instructed Barron and his team to put together a report on Tetro before the release.
Q. What did the report say?
A. That Tetro had some dangers, but that if used properly, we could be confident it wouldn't hurt the public.
Q. How much time did you give Barron and his team to conduct research?
A. As much time as they needed. There was no rush.
Q. But you issued the press release shortly thereafter?
A. Obviously, we needed to get news to our shareholders.
Q. Why?
A. Because we have a fiduciary duty to let them know when we have a breakthrough.
Q. Did Barron warn you of potential side effects?
A. Of course. It's Barron's job as a scientist to hedge. It's my job as an executive to maximize our value.
Q. Did you conduct enough research on Tetro?
A. I told Barron to do what needed to be done, and gave a massive budget for the research on the permeation or whatever -- the monkey tests. What more could we have done?

Page 15

Q. Were you confident Tetro was safe?
A. I was. I wouldn't have released the news if it wasn't safe.
Q. Can you describe your presentation at the town hall meeting last March?
A. Yes, Barron got fired and started spreading ludicrous lies, so we had a town hall to address his claims.
Q. What did Dr. Barron say?
A. Accused ED of poisoning the environment. Said we rushed tests. He had become a celebrity by pretending to be a whistleblower.
Q. What did you say at the town hall?
A. We were invited by the Nita City Council and the Nita Department of Natural Resources. Their staff told me they knew the truth. They said that Tetro wasn't a problem, but we needed to talk about it.
Q. How did you convey that to citizens?
A. I put together a PowerPoint with Tony Drummey and some other scientists to tell the townspeople the truth.
Q. How did that presentation go?
A. Fine. I think the vast majority of people believed us. Dozens of people came up to me after the meeting and told me not to give into the naysayers.
Q. Were the "naysayers" present?
A. Yes, Barron and McNamara made a big ridiculous stink.

Page 16

Q. What did they say?
A. Barron got up and said I had blood on my hands. Told me I couldn't hide the truth anymore. Told me he would make sure I paid for my "crimes."
(Witness hand gesturing quotation marks.)
Q. What about McNamara?
A. Sean was just trying to get some money talking about the cows and the damage. I said it wasn't the time or the place, and we could discuss privately.
Q. Had he mentioned the deaths of his cows before?
A. Yes, but coming from a known animal abuser, I didn't take it seriously.
Q. Did you know McNamara before this time?
A. Yes, we were professional acquaintances.
Q. Had McNamara complained to you personally?
A. Absolutely. A few years before regarding a sheen on his stream. We did research and made sure it didn't happen again. I am not sure how it was resolved. I had my field manager handle it.
Q. Do you believe Tetro had anything to do with the cows dying?
A. I hire very intelligent people to develop highly specialized products to maximize our market share. Before I send those products out into the field, I make sure they are as safe as humanly possible. That's how I felt about Tetro,

4 (Pages 13 to 16)

BARKLEY COURT REPORTERS

Page 17

and that's why I put it out there.
Q. So you don't believe--
A. I don't know what killed those cows, but it wasn't my product. We did the right testing, we took all the time in the world, we were cautious bringing Tetro to the market, and we complied with all our laws.
Q. After McNamara told you about the cows, what did you do?
A. We kept testing Tetro to make sure it was safe, and I ordered the polyterene or ethylene lining of the pit to be replaced strictly as a precaution. I did it as a good faith gesture.
Q. But you maintain you didn't cause the illnesses and deaths?
A. No, and Sean has no proof of that.

Page 18

DEPOSITION REPORTER'S CERTIFICATE

I hereby certify that the witness in the foregoing deposition named,

MK PHELPS,

was by me duly sworn to testify the truth, the whole truth, and nothing but the truth in the within-entitled cause; that said deposition was taken at the time and place therein stated; that the testimony of said witness was reported by me, Nirelle Higgins, a student court reporter, a disinterested person, and was taken down by me in stenotype and transcribed through computer-aided transcription; and that the pertinent provisions of the applicable code or rules of civil procedure relating to the notification of the witness and counsel for the parties hereto of the availability of the original transcript of deposition for reading, correcting, and signing have been complied with.

And I further certify that I am not of counsel or attorney for either or any of the parties to said deposition, nor in any way interested in the outcome of the cause named in said caption.

IN WITNESS WHEREOF, I have hereunto subscribed my hand August 7, YR-0.

Nirelle Higgins

Nirelle Higgins

Page 19

DECLARATION OF WITNESS

I, MK PHELPS, hereby declare that I have read the foregoing testimony, and the same is true and a correct transcription of my said testimony except as I have corrected.

MK Phelps

MK PHELPS

August 7, YR-0

Date

5 (Pages 17 to 19)

BARKLEY COURT REPORTERS

Exhibit 25

Deposition Transcript Barron

Page 1

IN THE UNITED STATES DISTRICT COURT FOR THE DISTRICT OF
NITA CITY, NITA
CIVIL DIVISION

SEAN MCNAMARA,)
Plaintiff,)
vs.) CAL: YR-2-CIV-10886
ENERGY DYNAMICS, INC.,)
Defendant.)

DEPOSITION OF MATT BARRON

Reported by: Nirelle Higgins, Student Court Reporter

Page 2

DEPOSITION OF MATT BARRON

BE IT REMEMBERED THAT, pursuant to notice, commencing at the hour of 2:00 p.m. thereof, at 120 Old Oak Lane, Nita City, Nita, before me, Nirelle Higgins, a student court reporter, there personally appeared:

MATT BARRON,

called for oral examination by counsel for Plaintiff, who, after having been duly sworn to tell the truth, the whole truth, and nothing but the truth, testified as follows:

---oOo---

Page 3

EXAMINATION

Q. Can you state your name?
A. Matt Barron.
Q. What is your current address?
A. 120 Old Oak Lane. I have a small farm there.
Q. Is the farm a business?
A. No, not really. I occasionally bring some produce to the farmers market - eggs once in a while.
Q. How long have you lived at 120 Old Oak?
A. The last two years or so.
Q. What is your current occupation?
A. I am a volunteer chemical analyst for Green Fellows.
Q. What is Green Fellows?
A. It's an organization dedicated to preventing chemicals from ruining the environment.
Q. What do you do for them?
A. They do investigations into corporations using illegal pesticides, chemical additives, industrial lubricants that just get dumped into local water sources.
Q. How do you help them specifically?
A. They give me samples from water sources -- animals that have died. They have me conduct chemical tests.
Q. Do you receive a salary?
A. No, I do not.
Q. Are you currently employed?

Page 4

A. At the moment, I am living off my savings and volunteering for Green Fellows.
Q. Can you describe your education?
A. I attended Stanford University for undergraduate school and majored in chemistry. I minored in political science to be a well-rounded student.
Q. What did you do after graduating?
A. Well, I didn't graduate at first.
Q. When did you leave school?
A. I left school after my junior year. I got an offer from a major pharmaceutical company to do research for them.
Q. Why did they offer you this job?
A. My professor used to be in their Research and Development Division, and I was his star student. I took the money and ran with it.
Q. Did you eventually get your degree?
A. After the research grant ran up, I went back and took classes to get my degree.
Q. When did you graduate?
A. I finally got my degree after two years working at the company for a year.
Q. I'm sorry, can you provide dates or--
A. Yes, my apologizes. I left after my junior year of college in June YR-18. Then, I worked at the company until January YR-16.

1 (Pages 1 to 4)

BARKLEY COURT REPORTERS

Page 5

Q. And after leaving the company?
A. Well, I made a ton of money, so I traveled for a while. Went to Argentina for six months. Then, eventually, my parents talked sense into me, and I got my degree.
Q. What did you do to get your degree?
A. I needed to do one more year, and I was a bit rusty, so I didn't get to graduate in May YR-15. I had to take summer school class, and then I just graduated in December YR-15.
Q. What class did you fail?
A. Dutch Art History.
Q. What class did you take in the summer?
A. Introduction to Public Speaking. I just wanted my credit so I could leave.
Q. Once you graduated, where did you get your first job?
A. I started working at the University of Arizona. They had a program where they were developing chemical and biochemical components to improve solar cells, growing algae, developing new photovoltaic cells.
Q. How long were you there?
A. I worked there from January YR-14 until May YR-13.
Q. Where did you go from there?
A. I was accepted into a chemical and bioengineering program at the University of California at Berkley.
Q. What did you study?
A. I had a mentor who was pushing me toward the petroleum industry, so I started studying petrochemical engineering.

Page 6

Q. When did you get your degree?
A. I got my masters in chemical engineering in YR-13.
Q. Where did you go after graduating?
A. I got hired by Energy Dynamics in their R&D Department straight out of graduate school.
Q. What led you to testify in the current case?
A. I was instrumental in developing Tetrohydrocore, and it's the biggest mistake I ever made.
Q. How do you mean?
A. It's a chemical I developed that's now going to destroy the environment wherever it's used.
Q. Why will it destroy the environment?
A. Because on the one hand, it's very toxic. On the other hand, it's amazing at what it does. It makes ED tons of money, improves their efficiency at natural gas fracturing sites, and boosted their stock price from the day it was announced.
Q. How does that destroy the environment?
A. When profits are up, they have absolutely no motivation to stop. Natural gas in Nita and elsewhere is like a mint, just printing money. So why would they ever stop?
Q. How did you develop the chemical?
A. I had a great team, tons of money from Energy Dynamics, and lots of time to work.

Page 7

Q. Who was part of your team?
A. I was the head of the team, since it was based on an idea I had in graduate school, and I had Pat Conway, a really bright mind from MIT, and Tony Drummey, who ended up taking my job and just keeps peddling this poison.
Q. It was just the three of you?
A. We had some research assistants, but the three of us ran the show and came up with most of the ideas.
Q. What was the idea you had?
A. The entire process of hydraulic fracturing wastes a lot. When chemicals and water are shot into the ground, creating these tiny cracks to release gas, a lot of that gas gets lost. I wanted to create a chemical that attaches to the gas and prevents it from being lost into the shale rock or the atmosphere as the gas is harnessed.
Q. How did you develop that product?
A. Well, I worked with Pat and Tony and others to come up with a formula, that for legal reasons, I can't discuss in detail, but let's just say it did the job.
Q. How?
A. In essence, the gas molecules that are released are only unlocked, so to speak, because you put them under extreme pressure. Well, that pressure can send those gas molecules where you don't want them to go. That's where Tetro comes into play.

Page 8

Q. So it prevents waste?
A. Exactly. Instead of losing some of the gas to Mother Nature, or the ground, we keep the lion's share.
Q. How big a breakthrough was this?
A. When I told MK Phelps we could increase efficiency by almost 30 percent, I thought she was going to cry. She started drafting the press release almost immediately, wanted to hype the product, get the stock prices up.
Q. When did you tell her?
A. I obviously kept her posted as the product developed, but we had our first major breakthrough in the spring of YR-4.
Q. What was the breakthrough?
A. For the first time, we were able to get Tetro to consistently and reliably bind to gas molecules. Before then, it was random. Some batches there'd be perfect bonding, sometimes they'd actively repel each other.
Q. When did you bring this to Phelps' attention?
A. We had a meeting on June 13, YR-4.
Q. How did she take the news?
A. She was ecstatic. She jumped out of her chair and said, "We're going to be the next Conoco Phillips." But there was an expletive in there. I'm sorry, I don't want to be vulgar.
Q. How did you explain this breakthrough?

2 (Pages 5 to 8)

BARKLEY COURT REPORTERS

Page 9

A. I told her we got it to do what we wanted, but we just had to make sure it didn't have the kind of negative consequences that often come with these innovations.
Q. What kind of negative consequences?
A. Chemists are sensitive to the notion we deal in dangerous toxins. Tetro itself is a derivative of sulfuric acid, which is extremely deadly even in small doses. I told Phelps we needed to do tests to see what this stuff would do.
Q. What did she say?
A. Her exact words were, "Don't be the buzz kill, Matt."
Q. How did the rest of the conversation go?
A. She told me my budget was whatever I needed, perform the tests, and bring her good news when I was ready.
Q. How did the test go?
A. Well, first we had to determine how much of this stuff would get out and not adhere to the gas we extracted. I needed to see if this stuff was going to go rogue.
Q. What conclusion did you reach?
A. Kind of inconclusive. We couldn't be sure it wouldn't get into aquifers and water sources in the area. I told them that. They didn't care.
Q. What other tests did you conduct?
A. We needed to test how easily this stuff got out into the environment. When the by-products of fracking come back up, they have to go somewhere. The process uses millions of

Page 10

gallons of water, and what comes back up with all the nasty chemicals and additives has to go somewhere.
Q. Where does it go?
A. Pits. They just dig them out of the ground, throw a tarp in there, and call it a day. I told them they needed very strong pits based on extreme danger of this chemical. They didn't listen.
Q. What would happen if Tetro escaped?
A. That was the last thing we tested. We gave lab animals relatively small doses of Tetro dissolved in their water and found some horrifying results. They had tumors, blindness, unexplained deaths, you name it, and these animals suffered from it.
Q. Did you warn Phelps?
A. I wrote my report. She chose not to listen.
Q. When did you provide this report?
A. Early YR-3, maybe January or February.
Q. What happened when they introduced Tetro into the field?
A. I quit. Phelps thinks she fired me, but I told her in no uncertain terms, I was out if they started using Tetro.
Q. What happened after you left?
A. I started a blog to publish the truth about this, started posts on Facebook to make sure people got the word out.

Page 11

Q. Is that how you got the attention of Green Fellows?
A. Yes, and others. I started doing interviews, talking with local news. It was all pretty exciting.
Q. Can you describe the town hall you attended?
A. Yes, it was March 8, YR-1. The town hall was called by ED to calm the people of Nita City down. They were riled up after my interviews.
Q. Who was there?
A. Phelps spoke, Drummey got up and gave a little speech about "safety" and "testing," but it was all a joke.
Q. What did you say?
A. I want to be polite, but I calmly told the people of the town that this chemical was going to cause major problems.
Q. What happened then?
A. Phelps told the whole room I'd been fired for inappropriate conduct.
Q. What kind of conduct?
A. Phelps didn't say in the meeting, but I think she was talking about my criticism of the company.
Q. Had you ever faced any other discipline from the company?
A. Some minor issues, but nothing serious.
Q. What issues?
A. I was given a one-day suspension for a physical

Page 12

altercation with Drummey.
Q. When did this occur?
A. About six months before I quit, so January YR-3. I quit that June.
Q. What was the altercation?
A. Drummey just pushed every single one of my buttons, and was saying I was being too cautious with testing and costing the company millions.
Q. How did it become physical?
A. He got too close to me, so I pushed him and knocked over some expensive equipment. I was suspended, but that was it.
Q. Getting back to the meeting, what else happened?
A. I really rattled Phelps' cage. The town was on my side. You could just feel it. Then, Sean McNamara jumped in and said he wasn't going to have it, and the chemicals were hurting his cows.
Q. Did you speak with McNamara after the meeting?
A. Yeah, Sean said there was a real problem here, wanted to know if I could help. I told him I wasn't sure what I could do.
Q. Why couldn't you help?
A. I'm not a vet, and I only know what we do in the lab. The lab results were bad, but I wasn't sure if they would absolutely, positively lead to health concerns in large

3 (Pages 9 to 12)

BARKLEY COURT REPORTERS

Page 13

mammals; not at that time at least.
Q. What happened after the town hall?
A. I kept raising the idea of this being a problem, started touring around Nita, beating the drums against ED.
Q. Has that been lucrative?
A. It pays the bills. My speaking fees are small. I'm not in this for the money. I'm in it for taking down this corporation that's intentionally hurting people.
Q. How do you know it's international?
A. When a team of scientists says, "This stuff is harmful," and you use it anyway, without further testing, and you barely protect the pits you're dumping it in from the elements, what else can you call that?
Q. What contact, if any, have you had with Phelps since the town hall?
A. I have sent Phelps emails explaining I'd love to have a public debate at some point over the values we want in our community. She never responds.

Page 14

DEPOSITION REPORTER'S CERTIFICATE

I hereby certify that the witness in the foregoing deposition named,

MATT BARRON,

was by me duly sworn to testify the truth, the whole truth, and nothing but the truth in the within-entitled cause; that said deposition was taken at the time and place therein stated; that the testimony of said witness was reported by me, Nirelle Higgins, a student court reporter, a disinterested person, and was taken down by me in stenotype and transcribed through computer-aided transcription; and that the pertinent provisions of the applicable code or rules of civil procedure relating to the notification of the witness and counsel for the parties hereto of the availability of the original transcript of deposition for reading, correcting and signing have been complied with.

And I further certify that I am not of counsel or attorney for either or any of the parties to said deposition, nor in any way interested in the outcome of the cause named in said caption.

IN WITNESS WHEREOF, I have hereunto subscribed my hand this July 28, YR-0.

Nirelle Higgins
Nirelle Higgins

Page 15

DECLARATION OF WITNESS

I, MATT BARRON, hereby declare that I have read the foregoing testimony, and the same is true and a correct transcription of my said testimony except as I have corrected.

Matt Barron
Signature

July 28, YR-0
Date

4 (Pages 13 to 15)

BARKLEY COURT REPORTERS

Deposition Transcript Castrigano

Page 1

IN THE UNITED STATES DISTRICT COURT
FOR THE DISTRICT OF NITA CITY, NITA
CIVIL DIVISION

SEAN MCNAMARA,)
Plaintiff,)
vs.) CAL: YR-2-CIV-10886
ENERGY DYNAMICS, INC.,)
Defendant.)

DEPOSITION OF LOGAN CASTRIGANO

Reported by: Nirelle Higgins, Student Court Reporter

Page 2

DEPOSITION OF LOGAN CASTRIGANO

BE IT REMEMBERED THAT, pursuant to notice, commencing at the hour of 11:00 a.m. thereof, at 2484 S. Bernadette Court, Nita City, Nita, before me, Nirelle Higgins, a student court reporter, there personally appeared:

LOGAN CASTRIGANO,

called for oral examination by counsel for Defendant, who, after having been duly sworn to tell the truth, the whole truth, and nothing but the truth, testified as follows:

---o0o---

Page 3

EXAMINATION

Q. Please state your name for the record?
A. Logan Castrigano.
Q. What is your address?
A. 2484 S. Bernadette Court.
Q. What is your current occupation?
A. I am Chief Legislative Advocate for the United States Natural Gas Consortium.
Q. What does that position entail?
A. I'm in charge of making sure job creators across the country are heard at the state, local, and federal level. It's my job to explain the Consortium's position to government officials.
Q. How long have you been in that position?
A. Since late last year. I joined their team in December YR-2.
Q. How did you get that job?
A. What do you mean?
Q. Well, let me ask what you did before joining the Consortium?
A. I was an environmental analyst with the Department of Natural Resources.
Q. And you were hired directly from the DNR?
A. I took a brief sabbatical after leaving the DNR.
Q. Can you describe your educational background?

Page 4

A. Yes, I have a masters in environmental studies from the University of Colorado. I was an organic chemistry major in college and got my bachelor of science from Colorado State.
Q. When did you get your bachelor's degree?
A. May of YR-18.
Q. What did you do after graduation?
A. I joined Teach for America.
Q. What subject did you teach?
A. Math and English.
Q. Did you have any positions related to science?
A. When I was done with Teach for America, I joined the Department of Natural Resources as a temp.
Q. What were your responsibilities?
A. Mainly administrative assistance, helping with filing, taking samples and reports to higher-ups from the lab we had.
Q. For how long were you with the DNR?
A. I was with the TFA for three years, and then I stayed with the DNR.
Q. Where did you go from the DNR?
A. I joined a masters program for environmental studies at University of Colorado in YR-6 -- September of YR-6.
Q. What did you study?
A. I studied a lot of topics over my two-year program, but I wrote a paper on environmental toxicology and risk

1 (Pages 1 to 4)

BARKLEY COURT REPORTERS

Page 5

management.

Q. Was it published?

A. It was never published.

Q. Have you written anything that has been published?

A. No, I have not.

Q. How are you involved in this case?

A. I was the inspector assigned to the property in question before McNamara brought the complaint.

Q. Can you describe your duties as an inspector?

A. Yes, it's pretty simple. It was my job to drive around the state where I was assigned and check out the well sites, dumping pits, and treatment plants.

Q. What else do you inspect?

A. I take water and soil samples from the surrounding areas.

Q. What were you checking the soil for?

A. Chemicals associated with fracturing and other by-products of the operation.

Q. What kind of by-products?

A. For one thing, the chemicals that get pumped into the ground are bad enough. Benzene and xylene are two chemicals we test for, but I also need to test the soil for TDS.

Q. What does that stand for?

A. TDS means total dissolved solids. Those are the natural products that come up from the soil. Essentially,

Page 6

salts and other compounds that can pollute the soil and water.

Q. What do you expect in water readings?

A. It depends on the chemicals we test for. Whether or not they've been labeled carcinogenic or not by the state.

Q. What chemicals are carcinogenic and which aren't?

A. There are literally hundreds of chemicals we test for at these sites, and I'd say, it breaks down about 50/50 between carcinogenic and noncarcinogenic.

Q. How do you, at the DNR, tell companies to handle the discharge?

A. Well, there are a lot of complex regulations that tell them how to handle the wastewater. Some sites are close enough to sewer treatment plants that they just send it right over. Others treat the water on site, and still, some others just dig out massive pits.

Q. What system did the site in question have?

A. The ED site we're discussing was not very close to any municipal treatment sites, so they opted for a pit.

Q. How do you enforce pit regulations?

A. Regular inspection and random testing of water levels, photographs being taken, making sure the pit is up to code.

Q. What happens if they aren't up to code?

A. The operator is fined, the citation goes into their permanent file and in my own for write-ups, and repeat

Page 7

offenders get punished.

Q. When did you become familiar with Tetrohydrocore?

A. ED came out with it three or four years ago. All I knew is it led to a boom in their profits.

Q. Did you know the chemical makeup of the compound?

A. No, these guys are pretty secretive about their compounds, and the law doesn't force them to disclose much.

Q. Did you ask anybody if it was carcinogenic?

A. The wheels turn pretty slowly at the state legislature, and it's their job to determine if this is a carcinogen or not.

Q. Did you run tests to see if Tetro was leaking out of the pits?

A. Sure, but I didn't know what levels would be appropriate since I wasn't sure what the chemical makeup was.

Q. How did you know how to detect it?

A. The State required ED to give us at least an indicator that attached to acid in the compound and identified its presence in water or soil.

Q. But you still did not know what it was?

A. No, but we knew when it was present.

Q. How often did you conduct random inspection?

A. I stated doing inspection for the DNR and learning the ropes in January of YR-5 when I was still earning my

Page 8

masters. It was basically an internship. I started by doing a few per month, and by the end, I did at least one a week.

Q. Is that because of the increase in activity?

A. Yes, and also because we were a bit understaffed.

Q. Was your work consistent?

A. What do you mean?

Q. I mean, did you have busy seasons, or lulls in activity?

A. I had a personal lull when I was suspended, but, otherwise, it was year-round.

Q. Why were you suspended?

A. I called an operator before inspecting to make an appointment.

Q. What operator?

A. It was an ED well a few miles west of the McNamara site.

Q. When was your suspension?

A. I was suspended a week in August YR-4.

Q. What were the most recent tests you performed on the site in question?

A. I performed tests on the McNamara site twice a year at random intervals every year I was with DNR.

Q. What trends did you notice in the samples and the site?

A. There were increased traces of Tetro once they

2 (Pages 5 to 8)

BARKLEY COURT REPORTERS

Page 9

introduced the chemical, and there were varying quantities of benzene and a few other carcinogens.
Q. Did you issue any citations in your time with them?
A. Only for the pit in May of YR-5.
Q. Why?
A. Because the tarp wasn't secured properly, and there was a high probability of spillover and seepage.
Q. Was that reflected in the samples you took?
A. Not at the time I was there. But, like I said, it was a possibility.
Q. Did you alert the company?
A. I issued the citation. So, yes, I did.
Q. Did you talk to anyone else about this?
A. I warned McNamara to keep an eye on his livestock and monitor them in case they got near the drinking water.
Q. Do you have a record of this conversation?
A. No, it was face-to-face.
Q. When?
A. Sometime in the summer of YR-5. Probably August when we got the test results back.
Q. What do you know about the toxicity of Tetro?
A. The results are inconclusive.
Q. Have you ever run any studies on it?
A. That's never been my job. I know Barron and Green Fellows have, but we know they reach their conclusions then

Page 10

try to justify them with bogus science.
Q. So what has been your job at the DNR?
A. My job was to monitor the levels of chemicals already identified as dangerous, go out into the field, and make sure corporations are complying with those guidelines. Also, it was a lot about issuing tickets to make money for the State.
Q. I'd like to talk about your reports of February YR-3, August YR-3, and February YR-2 -- your last report.
A. Okay.
Q. Starting with your February YR-3 report, can you describe your finding at the Old Reservation wells?
A. Yes, levels of carcinogenics were normal. The pit lining looked like it had been replaced since the citation. I took samples upstream and downstream to test the water for carcinogens. Neither tested positive for unacceptable levels of benzene, cadium, or the other carcinogens I screen for.
Q. Did you complete a report?
A. Yes, it's available publicly.
Q. Does your report reflect your findings?
A. Yes.
Q. For every chemical you test for?
A. For field investigations and random screenings we do "test screenings." These are basically tests to see if we

Page 11

need to do further, more in-depth tests. We don't preform additional tests for every chemical if the levels for indicator compounds aren't elevated.
Q. What are indicator compounds?
A. There are a few. Mainly benzene, xylene, and arsenic. Those are the three we test for.
Q. What about when you returned in August?
A. I went back to the site and performed the tests I had conducted in the past, but this time there seemed to be elevated levels of arsenic and benzene.
Q. Did you reflect that in your report?
A. I did. I note the levels as they were above the threshold that we can take as acceptable.
Q. Did you alert the company of those elevated levels?
A. The levels we observed weren't citation worthy in my opinion.
Q. Do you have discretion?
A. As an investigator, I did. There is a range for the levels of certain chemicals, and once you hit that range, you get to make a judgment call.
Q. What informed your judgment call?
A. I spoke with Tony Drummey at Energy Dynamics. He's a chemist and an old friend of mine.
Q. What did Drummey advise you?
A. That since the introduction of Tetro, there might be an

Page 12

elevated level. Drummey said the chemical they're using sometimes shows up in wastewater mimicking the compounds of arsenic and benzene.
Q. Did you speak with your own supervisors?
A. Yes, I wrote in my report what Drummey told me, and that was that.
Q. And did not issue a citation?
A. I probably wouldn't have anyway but wanted to find out more. I just followed up with them to be thorough.
Q. What about your final report in February YR-2?
A. Everything was normal. There had been an unusual thaw that winter, so the water level of the stream was high. As a result, the wastewater pit was closer to the stream than I would have liked, but I just noted that for future reference.
Q. What future action did you take?
A. None. Once the thaw runoff receded, the problem would be fixed. At worst, there'd be a temporary washout of minimal damage.
Q. Why did you leave the DNR?
A. I was released for failure to meet my quotas.
Q. What quotas?
A. Well, they're not official quotas, but my bosses released me for not writing enough citations. They said I was not doing my job. I said I couldn't force anyone to

3 (Pages 9 to 12)

BARKLEY COURT REPORTERS

Page 13

violate the law. We just saw things differently, so I left.
Q. You left, or they released you?
A. It doesn't matter to me. Really, I'm not too proud. I have a great job now, and I'm helping industry leaders bring jobs to Nita.
Q. Were you at the Nita City town hall on the night of March 8, YR-1?
A. I was but just to observe on behalf of my clients.
Q. Did you comment during the open mike phase?
A. I did. I thanked Phelps and ED for doing an amazing job and said they were always responsible during my time at DNR.
Q. Are they a client of yours?
A. Not directly.
Q. What do you mean?
A. Well, at the Consortium, we don't have ED as a direct client. We hope maybe someday, but for now, they just share common interests of exploration and bringing great jobs to Nita.

Page 14

DEPOSITION REPORTER'S CERTIFICATE

I hereby certify that the witness in the foregoing deposition named,

LOGAN CASTRIGANO,

was by me duly sworn to testify the truth, the whole truth, and nothing but the truth in the within-entitled cause; that said deposition was taken at the time and place therein stated; that the testimony of said witness was reported by me, Nirelle Higgins, a student court reporter, a disinterested person, and was taken down by me in stenotype and transcribed through computer-aided transcription; and that the pertinent provisions of the applicable code or rules of civil procedure relating to the notification of the witness and counsel for the parties hereto of the availability of the original transcript of deposition for reading, correcting, and signing have been complied with.

And I further certify that I am not of counsel or attorney for either or any of the parties to said deposition, nor in any way interested in the outcome of the cause named in said caption.

IN WITNESS WHEREOF, I have hereunto subscribed my hand this July 9, YR-0.

Nirelle Higgins

Nirelle Higgins

Page 15

DECLARATION OF WITNESS

I, LOGAN CASTRIGANO, hereby declare that I have read the foregoing testimony, and the same is true and a correct transcription of my said testimony except as I have corrected.

Logan Castrigano

Signature

July 9, YR-0

Date

4 (Pages 13 to 15)

BARKLEY COURT REPORTERS

Appendices

STATE OF NITA
ADMINISTRATIVE CODE

(20 NAC 25.001)

TITLE 20: Department of Natural Resources

CHAPTER 25: Oil and Natural Gas

(20 NAC 25.001)

Sec. 25.001. Declaration of Policy.

It is hereby declared to be in the public interest to foster, to encourage, and to promote the development, production, and utilization of natural resources of oil and gas in the state in such a manner as will prevent waste; to authorize and to provide for the operation and development of oil and gas properties in such a manner that a greater ultimate recovery of oil and gas be had and that the correlative rights of all owners be fully protected; and to encourage and to authorize cycling, recycling, pressure maintenance, and secondary recovery operations in order that the greatest possible economic recovery of oil and gas be obtained within the state to the end that the landowners, the royalty owners, the producers, and the general public realize and enjoy the greatest possible good from these vital natural resources.

REDACTED

(20 NAC 25.100)

Sec. 25.100. General Definitions.

When used in this Code, unless the context requires otherwise, the term:

1. "Abandoned pipeline" means an underground gathering pipeline that is no longer in service, is physically disconnected from in-service facilities, and is not intended to be reactivated for future use.
2. "Certificate of clearance" means a permit prescribed by the commission for the transportation or the delivery of oil or gas or product and issued or registered in accordance with the rule, regulation, or order requiring such permit.

3. "Commission" means the industrial commission.

4. "Field" means the general area underlain by one or more pools.

5. "Gas" means and includes all natural gas and all other fluid hydrocarbons not defined in this section as oil.

6. "Oil" means and includes crude petroleum oil and other hydrocarbons regardless of gravity which are produced at the wellhead in liquid form and the liquid hydrocarbons known as distillate or condensate recovered or extracted from gas, other than gas produced in association with oil and commonly known as casinghead gas.

****REDACTED****

21. "Reserve pit" means an excavated area used to contain drill cuttings accumulated during oil and gas drilling operations and mud-laden oil and gas drilling fluids used to confine oil, gas, or water to its native strata during the drilling of an oil and gas well.

22. "Underground gathering pipeline" means an underground gas or liquid pipeline that is designed for or capable of transporting crude oil, natural gas, carbon dioxide, or water produced in association with oil and gas which is not subject to chapter 49-22.

23. "Waste" means and includes:

    a. Physical waste, as that term is generally understood in the oil and gas industry.
    b. The inefficient, excessive, or improper use, or the unnecessary dissipation, of reservoir energy.
    c. The locating, spacing, drilling, equipping, operating, or producing of any oil or gas well or wells in a manner which causes, or tends to cause, reduction in the quantity of oil or gas ultimately recoverable from a pool under prudent and proper operations, or which causes or tends to cause unnecessary or excessive surface loss or destruction of oil or gas.

****REDACTED****

(20 NAC 25.800)

Sec. 25.800. Maintenance of Disposal Sites.

(a) *Preparation and implementation of plan.* Prior to generation of waste, the well operator shall prepare and implement a plan and site for the control and disposal of fluids, residual waste, and drill cuttings, including tophole water, brines, drilling fluids, additives, drilling muds, stimulation fluids, well-servicing fluids, oil, production fluids, and drill cuttings from the drilling, alteration, production, plugging, or other activity associated with oil and gas wells.

(b) *Requirements.* The plan must identify the control and disposal methods and practices utilized by the well operator and be consistent with this act and all other applicable acts.

(c) *Disposal pit maintenance.* Except as provided in § 78.60(b) and 78.61(b) (relating to discharge requirements; and disposal of drill cuttings), the operator shall contain pollutional substances and wastes from the drilling, altering, completing, recompleting, servicing, and plugging the well, including brines, drill cuttings, drilling muds, oils, stimulation fluids, well treatment and servicing fluids, and plugging and drilling fluids other than gases in a pit, tank, or series of pits and tanks. The operator shall install or construct and maintain the pit, tank, or series of pits and tanks in accordance with the following requirements:

(1) The pit, tank, or series of pits and tanks shall be constructed and maintained with sufficient capacity to contain all pollutional substances and wastes which are used or produced during drilling, altering, completing, and plugging the well.

(2) A pit shall be designed, constructed, and maintained so that at least two feet of freeboard remain at all times. If open tanks are used, the tanks shall be maintained so that at least two feet of freeboard remain at all times unless the tank is provided with an overflow system to a standby tank or pit with sufficient volume to contain all excess fluid or waste. If an open standby tank is used, it shall be maintained with two feet of freeboard. If this subsection is violated, the operator immediately shall take the necessary measures to ensure the structural stability of the pit or tank, prevent spills, and restore the two feet of freeboard.

(3) Pits and tanks shall be designed, constructed, and maintained to be structurally sound and reasonably protected from unauthorized acts of third parties.

(4) A pit or tank that contains drill cuttings from below the casing seat, pollutional substances, wastes, or fluids other than tophole water, fresh water, and uncontaminated drill cuttings shall be impermeable.

****REDACTED****

(b) The operator may request to use practices other than those specified in subsection (a) which provide equivalent or superior protection by submitting a request to the Department for approval. The request shall be made on forms provided by the Department.

(20 NAC 25.900(e))

Sec. 25.900(e) Protection of Water Sources.

(a) A well operator who affects a public or private water supply by pollution or diminution shall restore or replace the affected supply with an alternate source of water adequate in quantity and quality for the purposes served by the supply as determined by the Department.

(b) A landowner, water purveyor, or affected person suffering pollution or diminution of a water supply as a result of drilling, altering, or operating an oil or gas well may so notify the Department and request that an investigation be conducted. The notice and request must include the following:

(1) The name, address, and telephone number of the person requesting the investigation.

(2) The type, location, and use of the water supply.

(3) Available background quality and quantity data regarding the water supply, if known.

(4) Well depth, pump setting, and water level, if known.

(5) A description of the pollution or diminution.

(c) Within ten days of the receipt of the investigation request, the Department will investigate the claim and will, within forty-five days of receipt of the request, make a determination. If the Department finds that pollution or diminution was caused by the drilling, alteration, or operation activities or if it presumes the well operator responsible for polluting the water supply of the landowner or water purveyor under section 208(c) of the act (58 N.C. Stat. § 601.208(c)), the Department will issue orders to the well operator necessary to assure compliance with this section.

****REDACTED****

(f) *Quality*. The quality of a restored or replaced water supply will be deemed adequate if it meets the standards established under the Nita Safe Drinking Water Act (35 P. S. § § 721.1-721.17) or is comparable to the quality of the water supply before it was affected by the operator if that water supply did not meet these standards.

(g) *Adequate quantity*. A restored or replaced water supply will be deemed adequate in quantity if it meets one of the following as determined by the Department:

(1) It delivers the amount of water necessary to satisfy the water user's needs and the demands of any reasonably foreseeable uses.

(2) It is established through a connection to a public water supply system that is capable of delivering the amount of water necessary to satisfy the water user's needs and the demands of any reasonably foreseeable uses.

(3) For purposes of this paragraph and with respect to agricultural water supplies, the term "reasonably foreseeable" use includes the reasonable expansion of use where the water supply available prior to drilling exceeded the actual use.

(h) *Water source serviceability*. Replacement of a water supply includes providing plumbing, conveyance, pumping, or auxiliary equipment and facilities necessary for the water user to utilize the water supply.

(1) If the water supply is for uses other than human consumption, the operator shall demonstrate to the Department's satisfaction that the restored or replaced water supply is adequate for the purposes served by the supply.

(2) Tank trucks or bottled water are acceptable only as temporary water replacement for a period approved by the Department and do not relieve the operator of the obligation to provide a restored or replaced water supply.

(3) If the well operator and the water user are unable to reach agreement on the means for restoring or replacing the water supply, the Department or either party may request a conference under section 501 of the Act (58 N. Stat. § 601.501).

(20 NAC 25.980(a))

Sec. 25.980(a) Causes of Action.

(a) Nothing in this section shall be construed to impose on any owner, operator, or supervisor of a well operator or proprietor a higher duty of care than other owners and operators of similar businesses.

(b) Nothing in this section shall be construed to impose on any owner, operator, or supervisor of a well strict liability for damages caused to property or persons from well operations.

Appendix B

Jury Instructions

Preliminary Instructions Given Prior to the Evidence

1. You have been selected as jurors and have taken an oath to well and truly try this cause. This trial will last one day.

2. During the progress of the trial there will be periods of time when the Court recesses. During those periods of time, you must not talk about this case among yourselves or with anyone else. The attorneys are not allowed to speak with you, so do not attempt to do so.

3. You should keep an open mind. You should not form or express an opinion during the trial and should reach no conclusion in this case until you have heard all of the evidence, the arguments of the counsel, and the final instructions as to the law that will be given to you by the Court.

4. First, the attorneys will have an opportunity to make opening statements. These statements are not evidence and should be considered only as a preview of what the attorneys expect the evidence will be. Following opening statements, witnesses will be called to testify. They will be placed under oath and questioned.

5. It is counsel's right and duty to object where testimony or other evidence is being offered that he or she believes is not admissible. When the Court sustains an objection, the jurors must disregard the question, draw no inference, nor speculate as to what the answer would have been if the witness were allowed to answer. When the Court overrules an objection, the jurors must not give that evidence any different weight than if the objection had not been made.

6. At the conclusion of evidence of both sides, the attorneys will give closing arguments. Closing arguments are made by the attorneys to discuss the facts and circumstances in the case and should be confined to the evidence and to reasonable inferences to be drawn therefrom. Finally, just before you retire to consider your verdict, I will give you further instructions on the law that applies to this case.

Final Jury Instructions

THE COURT will now instruct you on the law governing this case.

1. You must arrive at a verdict by unanimous vote, applying the law as you are now instructed to the facts as you have observed and find them to be.

2. Plaintiff, Sean McNamara, has filed a claim against Defendant, Energy Dynamics, Inc., for negligence.

3. The Defendant denies the claim and also alleges Plaintiff was at fault for causing his own damage.

Negligence—Essential Factual Elements

4. Plaintiff claims that he was harmed by Energy Dynamics's negligence. To establish this claim, Plaintiff McNamara must prove all of the following:

   a. that Energy Dynamics was negligent;

   b. that Sean McNamara was harmed; and

   c. that Energy Dynamics negligence was a substantial factor in causing Plaintiff McNamara's harm—that is, but for the negligence the damage would not have occurred.

Basic Standard of Care

5. Negligence is the failure to use reasonable care to prevent harm to oneself or to others. A person can be negligent by acting or by failing to act. A person is negligent if he or she does something that a reasonably careful person would not do in the same situation or fails to do something that a reasonably careful person would do in the same situation.

6. You must decide how a reasonably careful person would have acted in both Plaintiff's and Defendant's situation.

Comparative Fault

7. Defendant Energy Dynamics claims that Plaintiff McNamara's own negligence contributed to his harm. To succeed on this claim, Energy Dynamics must prove both of the following:

   a. that Sean McNamara was negligent; and

   b. that Sean McNamara's negligence was a substantial factor in causing his harm.

   If Energy Dynamics proves the above, Sean McNamara's damages are reduced by your determination of the percentage of Sean McNamara's responsibility. I will calculate the actual reduction.

Damages

   {NB: If damages are to be determined in another proceeding, read the following instruction; otherwise, continue with the below Compensatory Damage Instruction[s]}

8. You need not concern yourself with damages at this time.

   OR

9. Damages—Compensatory Damages

   a. If you decide that Sean McNamara has proved his claim against Energy Dynamics, Inc., you also must decide how much money will reasonably compensate Sean McNamara for the harm. This compensation is called "damages."

   b. The amount of damages must include an award for each item of harm that was caused by Energy Dynamics, Inc.'s wrongful conduct, even if the particular harm could not have been anticipated.

   c. Sean McNamara does not have to prove the exact amount of damages that will provide reasonable compensation for the harm. However, you must not speculate or guess in awarding damages.

Concluding Instruction

10. Ladies and Gentlemen of the jury, this is the conclusion of the instructions. It is now time to retire to the jury room where you will choose a foreperson and begin your deliberations. This is the verdict form, and upon making your decision, please fill out the form, sign, and date it, and then return with your verdict to the courtroom.

THE U.S. DISTRICT COURT
FOR THE DISTRICT OF NITA CITY, NITA
Civil Division

SEAN MCNAMARA,	)	
	)	
Plaintiff,	)	
	)	
v.	)	
	)	CAL: YR-2-CIV-10886
ENERGY DYNAMICS, INC.,	)	
	)	
Defendant.	)	

We, the Jury, return the following verdict, and each of us concurs in the verdict:

[Choose the appropriate verdict]

We, the Jury, unanimously find as follows in response to the questions submitted to us:

Question 1: Was Defendant Energy Dynamics negligent?

YES____________________ NO____________________

Question 2: Was Defendant Energy Dynamics's negligence a substantial factor in causing harm to Plaintiff Sean McNamara?

YES____________________ NO____________________

Question 3: Was Plaintiff Sean McNamara negligent?

YES____________________ NO____________________

Question 4: Was Plaintiff Sean McNamara's negligence a substantial factor in causing his harm?

YES____________________ NO____________________

Question 5: What percentage of responsibility for Plaintiff Sean McNamara's harm do you assign to each of the following?

Defendant Energy Dynamics	________%
Plaintiff Sean McNamara	________%
Total:	100%

Question 6: What is the amount of Plaintiff's total damages? __________

_______________ _______________________________

DATE FOREPERSON

CPSIA information can be obtained
at www.ICGtesting.com
Printed in the USA
BVHW020201291222
655232BV00010B/243

9 781601 568359